Into the Mountain

Into the Mountain
hostaged by the Abu Sayyaf

JOSE TORRES JR.

Edited,
with an Introduction,
by John Nery

CLARETIAN PUBLICATIONS

INTO THE MOUNTAIN
hostaged by the Abu Sayyaf

Copyright © 2001 by **Claretian Publications**
A division of Claretian Communications, Inc.
U.P. P.O. Box 4, Diliman 1101 Quezon City, Philippines
TE: 921-3984 • FAX: 921-6205
E-mail: claret@cnl.net
Website: http://www.bible.claret.org

Claretian Publications is a pastoral endeavor of the Claretian Missionaries in
the Philippines. It aims to promote a renewed spirituality rooted in the process
of total liberation and solidarity in response to the needs, challenges and pastoral demands of the Church today.

RESEARCH: Iris Cecilia Gonzales

COVER DESIGN: Edwin Reyes, cmf

ISBN 971-501-904-8

To the children of Basilan
— Muslim and *Christian*

Author's Note

THIS STORY IS NOT FICTION. Every character is flesh and blood, every incident a fact, every village a cartographic reality, every quotation a faithful transcription from the narratives of witnesses and participants.

This is a story of a people caught in a web of conflict and prejudice. This is a story they themselves compose and narrate. This is a story that has a beginning somewhere in history and an end—I hope—sometime in the near future. This is a continuing saga, of a people caught in a situation not of their doing, where victim becomes villain and villain turns victim.

This narrative is only a small fragment of a huge, unfinished picture. I hope, however, that the story it tells will open the reader's eyes to a wider reality, to an understanding of the battle that is continuously being waged, both literally and literarily, in Mindanao.

In the late 1980s, when I went home to Mindanao, my Muslim friends told me that if I wanted to become a successful journalist, I should study Islam and understand the religion by heart, because it would become the "wave of the future." I tried and failed.

When I met my friends again, they were already talking about *mujahedeens* who were to liberate Mindanao from "the clutches of oppression." They also told me about a phantom about to haunt the whole island and drive the oppressors away. They told me about the "Abusayap," a group of young idealistic Muslims which, my friends told me, was partly a military creation.

There's my story at last, I told myself. I did my research, went to the area, read books on Islamic revivalism, and talked to both Muslim leaders and ordinary citizens. I wrote news stories as I tried to fathom what the name Abu Sayyaf meant. I tried to understand the phenomenon of Islamic revivalism as I wrote about how bandit leaders and military officials rode together in military vehicles while ordinary soldiers and bandits killed each other in the battle zone.

Many branded my stories "incredible." A few years later, however, came vindication, when an Abu Sayyaf bandit and some government officials confessed that there was, indeed, collusion between them. But by then it was too late. The phantom had become a monster that killed, not for freedom nor for religion, but for money.

I went back to Mindanao and stayed in Basilan for a few months. Again I talked to as many people as I could, both Muslim and Christian, and they told me their fears. Both peoples had become victims, hostaged not only by the Abu Sayyaf but also by a government that offers solutions to nonexistent problems.

I was tempted to come out and tell a story based on my perception of the reality I saw, only to realize that analysis has been done already. Any new attempt to analyze the situation will only diminish reality. Again, I tried to look at the situation from the eyes of religion, from Islam and Christianity; I felt inadequate. But when I listened and let the people and their own experience speak, I found I could breathe.

This was not an easy story to write because I did not think about it. I just let the pieces fall; I just let the material flow. I did try to provide some context, but still in a story-driven format, through the three "intercessionals" that spiral inside the main narrative.

This is not an expose. This is a story. I would like this book to be read as a story because, as the Italian biographer Paco Ignacio Taibo II would say, only then may it be understood. I tried my best, and may have in many instances failed, *not* to explain the meaning of the narrative or the consequences of the incidents, to allow the reader to look for them. I would, however, warn the faithful reader not to look for meaning where there is none.

Central to the narrative is the life of Father Rhoel Gallardo, a young Claretian missionary who was killed, many say martyred, by the Abu Sayyaf. His death inspired a lot of people, especially religious and missionaries, well-meaning people all, from around the world. Here was a man willing to die for his faith, ready to give up his life for others, a very rare man in a selfish age.

I am bound to point out, however, that Father Rhoel's death also inspired some Christians to take up arms and kill fellow human beings "to defend the faith." To some degree, his death fuelled a cycle of violence that has ruled too many parts of the world in recent history.

In the end, this is a story about faith, the faith of a people on an island—nay, in a nation—which has been held hostage by circumstances that bred the Abu Sayyaf. I hope the reader will read it with the eyes of faith, a faith that is rooted in understanding.

We have nothing to lose if, to paraphrase the psalmist, we walk with the people into the mountain by listening to their story. Maybe we will find salvation there.

Jose Torres Jr.
July 28, 2001

ACKNOWLEDGEMENTS

The idea to come out with a book on Father Rhoel Gallardo's ordeal was first brought up by Father James Castro, cmf. When we got the nod of the Claretian congregation's Philippine province, off I went to Basilan where the missionaries welcomed me like a brother.

A lot of people made my journey "into the mountain" possible. Among them are former Basilan Bishop Romulo de la Cruz (for the tips, advise, food and bumpy rides to the mountains); Father Nestor Banga (for believing in me and for giving me access to "Sunrise Hotel"); Father Edgar Zamudio (for everything, but most especially for being there to guide me to Him during the most memorable Holy Week of my life); Father Loi Nacorda (for making me believe in miracles); Brother Arnel Alcober (for bringing me down to earth and showing me Teheman); Father Jojo Borja (for the "secret" stories of Basilan); Father Danny Deloso (for being there); Father Martin Jumuad (for the round-trip ticket); Father Noel Daduya (for the bowling competition); Brothers Sam and Pablo (for the company); Manang Lourdes (for taking care of me); and Manang Dolor (for reading the signs on my palm).

Also, Ms. Joy Granados (thanks for the allowance!); Dr. and Mrs. Alejandro Infante (for history, lunch, and hot sardines); Mr. and Mrs. Feria (for the Malamawi experience, among others); the Army's 32nd Infantry Battalion, especially Cpl. Repe, Pfc. Labaste, Pfc, Bendanilla (for forcing me to stay fit and for teaching me to hit the target); the CAFGUs of Tumahubong (for the security); the teachers of Claret Schools of Tumahubong and Maluso (for the laughter); the Sisters (for the prayers); the Bajaus of Teheman (for sharing with me their "waterworld"); Dodoy (salamat sa motor!); and Yvette (salamat sa paglaba!).

I also wish to thank Mr. Dan Mariano and the staff of abs-cbnNEWS.com; Leanne, Maritess, and Glenda of Newsbreak; the Philippine Center for Investigative Journalism; Howie Severino; the Philippine Daily Inquirer, Mindanao bureau; Julie Alipala-Inot; and Jules Benitez. Philippine Alliance of Human Rights Advocates; Anak Mindanao; Djay (for the contingency plan), Philippine News and Features, especially Sophie and May (who believed in me during those early years of the Abu Sayyaf); Tess Adora (salamat sa tiyaga!); John Nery (editor and friend); Iris Gonzales (for the invaluable research); and to my Muslim friend Mujib, without whom I would have not met the phantoms of Basilan.

To all of you, my deepest gratitude.

Litany

Hostages abducted by the Abu Sayyaf on March 20, 2000

Teachers

Claret School of Tumahubong
Father Rhoel Gallardo, cmf – school director, died May 3, 2000
Marissa Rante – rescued May 3, 2000
Reynaldo Rubio – rescued May 3, 2000
Anabelle Mendoza – died May 3, 2000
Wenifer Silorio – released March 23, 2000

Sinangkapan Elementary School
Teresita Academia – released July 2000
Rosebert and Lydda Ajon – rescued May 3, 2000
Eduardo Enriquez – beheaded April 19, 2000
Editha Lumame – died May 3, 2000
Erlinda Manuel – released July 2000
Albert Sahao – released March 20, 2000

Sinangkapan National High School
Dante Uban – beheaded April 19, 2000
Rodolfo Irong – rescued May 3, 2000
Ruben Democrito – died May 3, 2000

Tumahubong Central Elementary School
Juanito Arellano – school principal, released March 25, 2000
Nurhaida Katoh – released March 25, 2000
Saida Sahirin – released March 25, 2000
Nita Abajud – released March 25, 2000
Macario Mandun – released March 25, 2000
Abubakar Denil – released March 25, 2000
Sahijain Saijan – released March 25, 2000
Haiba Muslimin – released March 25, 2000

Students

Tumahubong Central Elementary School

Romela Mendoza – rescued May 3, 2000
Ian Rey Lucip – released July 2000
Ryan Laputan – released July 2000
Jul Padrique – released July 2000
Adolf Von Cijalvo – released April 7, 2000
Juliet Tonghay – released April 7, 2000
Jennelyn Emo – rescued May 3, 2000
Criselda Silvano – rescued May 3, 2000
Ricardo "Kipyong" Gregorio – rescued May 3, 2000
Chary Vergara – rescued May 3, 2000
Cristy Vergara – rescued May 3, 2000
Maria Cristina Francisco – rescued May 3, 2000
Christinly Diva – rescued May 3, 2000
Billy James Lariosa – released July 2000
Reylios Pia – released July 2000
Joselle Jane De La Torre – released July 2000
Hazel De La Torre – released July 2000
Nova Verallo – released April 14, 2000
Lani Mae Cachuela – released April 14, 2000
Emelyn Cachuela – rescued May 3, 2000
Darrel Chris Reambonanza – released March 25, 2000
Cristano Reambonanza III – released March 25, 2000
Rizzaline Reambonanza – released March 25, 2000
Joan Barnido – rescued May 3, 2000
Dana Rose Mijal – released March 25, 2000
Danne Rose Mijal – released March 25, 2000
Noraydah Umangkat – released March 25, 2000

Three students, children of Abu Sayyaf members, were abducted by mistake; they were released on March 25, 2000.

INTRODUCTION

JOE TORRES WENT TO BASILAN to write about a man; he came back with a book about an island.

I remember the first time he told me about the possibility. We were killing time at the newsroom of the now-defunct *Post*, the next day's issue already safely in bed. "The Claretians are thinking about putting out a book on Father Rhoel Gallardo," he said. [The missionary hostage had just been found dead.] "I'm thinking of doing it," he added.

He received the commission from Claretian Communications sometime in May last year. The following June, after the details of the assignment had been agreed on, he asked me to edit the book—an invitation, incidentally, that I would have forced from him if he had not obliged. (I must note that, in keeping with the technological spirit of our increasingly convergent times, he sent his request, at a time when we happened to be thousands of miles apart, by text.)

He finally found time to focus on the book in February this year, after the post-*Post* paper he worked for closed shop too. (That brings his career total of now-defunct newspapers to four, double mine, unless we consider the *Times*, during the hundred days it was managed by the editors who eventually got fired, as another paper with a distinct beginning and end. Newspapering, to put it mildly, is not a stable profession.)

Joe spent more than two months in Basilan, a troubled province he knows well, to do the legwork. Once, he called me from the island to schedule the editing; I think it was only the third time since the conversation in the newsroom that we discussed the book in some detail. I continued to think the book was a biography of Father Rhoel, the pre-eminent hostage of the March 20, 2000 kidnappings, although I did sense during that call that the material was on the verge of breaking out and taking over.

When I finally read the first pages of the manuscript, late in June this year, I was blown away. With remarkable intuition, Joe had divined exactly where the real story lay. It lay in *story*—that is, in the narratives of the witnesses and participants, in the re-telling and detailing of the protagonists (literally, *agon* being Greek for struggle).

Father Rhoel continues to be central to the main narrative, but the story has become that of the people themselves: Dolor the blind seer, Angie the catechist, Kipyong the man-child, Chary the teenager, Lydda the wife, Mr. Rubio the principal, Bendah the soldier, Romy the bishop, even Father Loi the survivor. The story is now also the account of Wenifer, who lost her baby; Marissa, who was abused; Nelson and Dante, who were beheaded; Anabelle and Editha and Ruben and Father Rhoel, who died while being "rescued." Through the anecdotal situationers he calls "intercessionals," Joe has even managed to include other Basilan voices—Abu Sayyaf urban assassin Ahmad Sampang and Christian vigilante Kumander Leleng among them—in the developing story.

The result is a book about Basilan—beautiful, tragic, emblematic.

THE STORIES IN THESE PAGES are fragmentary, impressionistic, incomplete—but they are "fraught with background," to use Erich Auerbach's seminal phrase. They can be understood in themselves, very much like scenes from a movie. But they can also be understood in relation to each other, as parts of a whole, as elements in a continuing headline-grabbing story, as moments in the stop-start struggle for inter-religious dialogue, as unforgettable stories in faith experience.

The background deepens because of Joe's habit of layering a story. He tells it once, perhaps obliquely; he tells it a second time, in another chapter, maybe this time directly; he mentions it again, a third time, briefly.

The extraordinary (and still unfinished) narrative of Father Loi Nacorda, to give one example, weaves in and out of three chapters: first as part of the retelling of Father Rhoel's mountaintop experience; next as seen through the memories of an Abu Sayyaf bandit, made edgy by the prospect of dying; last as a violent fast-forward to the most recent events.

In each instance, Father Loi is taken on his own terms. The same goes for all the witnesses—thus putting, say, an eighteen-year-old Grade 4 student on equal footing with a missionary bishop bodyguarded by an armed escort of thirty.

That we don't see this mix as something new is a tribute to the strength of the literary tradition called *sermo humilis*, from which this book derives.

Uppity classicists had taken their cue from the ancient Greeks: Tragedy was a function of nobility, of high social status. Stories about the lower classes were by definition necessarily either comedy or farce. The demotic language of Christianity, however, broke down this separation of styles. Beginning with the Christ-story itself, potent with what Auerbach called "its ruthless mixture of everyday reality and the highest and most sublime tragedy," a new "low style" emerged, finding dignity in the ordinary.

"Christ had not come as a hero and king but as a human being of the lowest social station," Auerbach writes in *Mimesis*. "His first disciples were fishermen and artisans; he moved in the everyday milieu of the humble folk of Palestine; he talked with publicans and fallen women, the poor and the sick and the children. Nevertheless, all that he did and said was of the highest and deepest dignity, more significant than anything else in the world."

These book's stories about "the poor and the sick and the children" of Basilan also derive from yet another Christian tradition of story-telling—one that goes as far back as Stephen, the first Christian who died for his faith. It is the tradition of faith stories giving witness to the persecution of martyrs (martyr being rooted in the Greek for witness).

This is not to say that the narrative now in your hands is religious in intent, only that "giving witness" is at the heart of it.

BASILAN TODAY is an island in extremis. At the turn of the 21st century, it is undergoing a test almost Biblical in its severity. It has spawned a many-headed monster called the Abu Sayyaf; it has also bred Father Rhoel and other martyrs. The choices its people face are as stark as good and evil, but their story is no medieval morality play. It is an absurdist drama, as vexing as a windowless cell, or *Manang* Dolor's bed, or the human heart.

John Nery
Philippine Daily Inquirer

WHEN THEY SAW the armed men in the middle of the road, blocking their way, it was already too late. The jeep was running downhill and there was no stopping it in time. The old man driving the vehicle slowed it down, but the armed men had already aimed their guns.

The first volley of fire hit the windshield, breaking the silence of the early morning. The driver changed gears and drove the jeep backwards. Another round, and the man sitting beside the driver slumped. Then the driver too. The shooting stopped only when the jeep came to a standstill.

"Mangadye 'ta (Let us pray)," the woman sitting behind the driver said. She took out her rosary. "Let us pray because they will kill us all."

"No, let's run!" another passenger, a young man, said.

"Our Father in heaven, holy be your name, your kingdom come, your will be done," the woman started.

The shooting started again as the armed men marched toward the vehicle. Bullets felled the young man who was trying to jump from the jeep.

The others continued praying.

Someone was hit, then another. The driver, who was still alive, shouted. "Cover yourselves!" There was blood all over the vehicle.

"Let's keep praying," the woman encouraged her companions. She used her body to try to cover a young woman sitting in front of her. (The attempt worked; the young woman was the massacre's lone survivor.)

The firing stopped. The armed men peered inside the vehicle. The wounded passengers were still praying.

The rifles spit fire again. Then there was silence.

One of the armed men approached the vehicle. He took out a big bolo called a barong and hacked away at the passengers. He wanted to make sure everyone was dead.

It was Valentine's Day, 1999.

ON THE NIGHT *before the massacre, the woman who would pray the rosary as she lay dying sang the responsorial psalm during the anticipated Mass in their village.*

Afterwards, the priest congratulated her for the "great performance," and teased her about the new dress she was wearing. "Don't worry, Father. I will never wear this again," the woman answered in kind.

She had been a village catechist for nine years. With her daughter, she had helped Christians in their village prepare for baptism, confirmation, weddings, even deaths. They also helped other villagers, especially women, earn through livelihood projects.

The woman needed to attend an Alay Kapwa seminar the next day in the city and had to travel almost seventy kilometers over a rugged highway. Her daughter wanted to go with her, but the priest said there was no more place for her in the vehicle.

"Don't worry," the priest said. "They will come back immediately."

That night, after the Mass, the mother went to her daughter's house.

"Why did you come, Nanay? You have to leave at four in the morning. It's already nine," the worried daughter said.

"I just want to see you," the mother said, hugging her daughter tight.

"Nay, you're so sentimental!" She was not used to her mother's display of affection.

"I don't have a jacket for tomorrow," the mother said.

"You can use mine," the daughter offered.

"No, don't worry. Yours is new. It might get ruined."

"Nay, it's all right. Even if it gets ruined, I won't mind because it's you using it," the daughter insisted. She handed her mother a P100 bill for her to buy food in the city, but the older woman did not accept the money.

"Don't worry. I will be back immediately," the mother said.

EARLY THE NEXT MORNING, at around 5 a.m., the daughter passed by her mother's house on her way to church, where it was her turn to read the responsorial psalm. When she reached the house, her father told her Nanay had already left for the city with the other catechists. The daughter decided to go back home, where she saw her husband preparing coffee in the kitchen.

She went inside the bedroom and kissed her small daughter. From the window, she saw a woman running toward the house. It was her aunt, crying.

"The priest's jeep was ambushed!" the woman said, panting.

"But who will ambush the priest's jeep?" the daughter asked, unbelieving. "Relax, auntie."

"It's true. All the passengers are dead," the older woman wailed.

The young woman went out of the house and ran to the church to get more news. Along the way she heard people saying: "You said she was killed? Why is she here?"

It was then that she started crying. People had mistaken her for her mother.

She heard people talking, saying everyone was dead.

The Mass started, but she could not read the responsorial psalm. She was crying in a corner of the church when the priest fetched her and seated her in front.

"Shhh," he said. "If they survive, you are the one who will die because you cry like there's no tomorrow," the priest teased his friend.

In the middle of the Mass, just as the priest raised the bread and the wine for consecration, the jeep that had taken the dead bodies from the ambush site arrived. The people laid the bloody, muddied bodies on the ground, outside the church door.

The priest went on with the Mass, even as the people started crying and wailing.

Someone had survived the ambush, the rumors spread quickly. The daughter prayed and hoped that it was her mother. She continued paying attention to the priest, although people were already standing and milling around the corpses outside.

"Look at them! Look what they did to the bodies," the young woman heard people saying. It was the last thing she heard, before she lost consciousness.

When she woke up, her father was hugging her. She looked around her. People inside the church were all crying, including the priest.

"I could not accept that my mother had died," she said much later. Even during the wake, she did not go near her mother's coffin. When she finally saw the jacket she had lent her mother the previous night, it bore bullet holes all over.

Outside the church, the young woman saw men laughing. She recognized some of them. They were her neighbors.

CHAPTER 1

IT IS DOLOR'S FATE to see what is coming, but forever remain helpless to do anything about it.

These days, regret would sometimes overwhelm her: at not being able to stop her own friends from getting killed, at not having told them the truth when they were still alive, at not telling anyone that the sign she saw on the palm of the soldier and on the palm of the priest were the marks of death, their own death sentence.

She had, in fact, met the soldier through the priest. But she did not actually see him, because she has been blind since birth.

On March 16, 2000, young Claretian missionary Rhoel Gallardo happened to be in Isabela, the capital of Basilan province. He stopped by to see her, and to ask her to go back with him to Tumahubong, in Sumisip town, where he was parish priest of the San Vicente Ferrer Parish, for a mercy mission.

Father Rhoel, who was barely a year into his Basilan assignment, was both Dolor's friend and patient. She had earlier found that he was suffering from arthritis, and after an hour-long massage using a commercial liniment, had cured him. Or so Father Rhoel liked to claim. He convinced the blind woman to share her gift and visit his village to help his poor parishioners, many of whom had not seen a doctor all their life.

"*Bien bueno gente gayot ele. Ta prepara le kape para comigo y ele gayot ta serve* (He was a good man. He used to make coffee for me and serve it personally)," Dolor later recalled.

That day, Dolor said yes and went with the priest. The bumpy jeep ride on a long, tortuous, ambush-prone road

**A
SENSE
OF
THINGS
TO
COME**

through the mountains took nearly four hours. The distance was seventy kilometers, more or less.

In the convent at the back of the small church in Tumahubong, she healed the sick until the wee hours of the morning. Even the soldiers of the Philippine Army's 10th Infantry Battalion who were stationed at a nearby camp came to ask Dolor to heal them or to read their future.

One of the soldiers asked Dolor to look at him because he was always feeling weak, especially in the evening.

"Show me your hand first," she said.

What she saw made her shiver. It was a familiar sign, something she had first seen over a year before, just a few days before catechists on their way to an Alay Kapwa seminar in Isabela walked into a massacre on Valentine's Day.

Dolor observed the same intensity, the same hue of red, on the palm of the soldier. Last year her inner eye had seen it on a young woman's hand; the young woman's mother was later hacked to death in the February 14 massacre.

"You have the sign. Be very careful," she warned the soldier. "I can feel the lines of your palm. At least two groups will do something bad."

"Stop it, *Manang*," the soldier answered. "I'm not into that."

Dolor sensed the fear in the man.

"I want you to take the pain from my back. I don't want you reading my palm," he snapped.

"But I can't tell what's wrong with your body if I don't first look at your palm. Through its lines I can tell if you are sick or not."

"What happened?" Father Rhoel jumped in. He had heard the heated exchange from the kitchen where he was preparing dinner.

"I was telling him that something is going to happen and he would be there to witness it, but he got angry," Dolor replied.

"Where would it happen, Dolor? Here? Are the bandits finally coming to get us?" the priest asked in jest.

"I don't know, Father. But it will be near where this soldier will be," she answered. Then, turning to the soldier, Dolor said: "You have other problems on your mind, but before you can resolve them, the two groups will come."

The priest asked the soldier where he was stationed. "I was transferred to Tipo-Tipo this week, Father," the man answered. Tipo-Tipo is a town fifteen kilometers from Tumahubong, populated mainly by Muslims.

"Your problem will just be nearby," Dolor told the soldier. "You are afraid, I know. I pity you because you are *cobardon*," she teased him.

The soldier angrily turned around and left in a hurry.

"What is *cobardon*, *Manang*?" the priest asked when he was alone with her.

"It means coward," Dolor explained. "I told the soldier that he is a coward. But he did not understand what *cobardon* is because he is not Chavacano."

"If he understood, he could have hurt you. You insulted him," Father Rhoel said.

"But he is supposed to be brave, Father. He is a soldier," Dolor answered. "Anyway, I told him the truth. Why would he be afraid to know the truth?"

The priest was silent. "Let's eat, *Manang*," he finally said.

The priest led the woman to the kitchen where she smelled the newly cooked rice on the table beside the fried fish and instant noodles the priest had prepared. The two ate in silence.

After the meal, Dolor resumed her session with the people who were gathered outside the convent under the avocado tree. From the sound of it, they seemed to be enjoying the cold evening breeze while waiting for their turn. It was Friday, March 17.

DOLOR HAS BEEN BLIND since birth, but she can read the destiny of men written on the palm of their hands. She is a passionate woman who loves to sing, always swaying her long black hair to the beat.

She speaks with utter sincerity, although she does not lack the humor that seems to come naturally when one lives on an island where people pass the time exchanging jokes or drinking coconut wine. Nothing seems to irk her, not even the banter of the men, mostly soldiers and militiamen, who lust after her still-shapely, fortysomething body.

Her hands, smooth as silk, possess healing powers that have baffled doctors who tried to test her curative ability. Politicians, soldiers, rebels, nuns, priests, and even the bishop respect her. They—who seem much older and wiser—often seek her words of simple wisdom.

"I can't believe these people. They believe in me," she would complain, especially during those long nights when, for lack of nothing to do, almost everybody in the neighborhood would go to her house on a hill and ask her to feel the lines on their palm, massage their neck, or fashion an amulet for their children. She would barely have enough time to sneak in a glass of milk for dinner.

"I want to help," she would always say. "But I don't know what to do. I touch them and I feel their pain," she would add, "and they would tell me that I healed them of their infirmities."

The priests and nuns on the island trusted the blind woman. They would seek her out for counsel during those times when they felt the burden was heavy and it was hard to move forward.

She was thirteen when she first saw the bearded man she later would claim to be Jesus Christ. She was not surprised that the Lord would visit her even in her sleep. It was no instant miracle, she would tell friends later. "I sweated to get God's attention," she said.

Ever since she was young, even before she could memorize the way to church, God was Dolor's only refuge. She constantly visited the "house of the bearded man" even though she had no idea what the structure looked like. She said she simply felt comfortable inside the small chapel, listening to the singing of the birds which never seemed to stop hopping from one wooden beam to another, savoring the sweet smell that came from the coconut oil lamp near the tabernacle.

The blind child would envy the other children she heard playing outside. She used to cry often and complain to the Lord why she could not see. She never got an answer, but she continued to hope. Every time she attended the Flores de Mayo, she would sit in a corner and smell the flowers offered to the Blessed Virgin Mary. "I might not enjoy their color but I love their smell," she would tell the other children. She would sing *Dios Te Salve* as the children marched to the altar to offer their flowers.

Father Jose Maria Querexeta, a Claretian missionary expelled from China when the communists took power, became Dolor's father, adviser, and friend after they met inside the church one April afternoon.

The priest found Dolor crying in the first pew of the chapel. "*Hija*, what is your name?" the priest asked. "Why are you crying?"

"My name is Dolor. I am blind. I want to ask the Lord if he can give me even just one good eye so I can see the birds," Dolor answered.

"What a beautiful name," the priest said. "Don't cry, my child. Go near the Blessed Sacrament and pray there. Jesus can hear you there."

She followed the priest's advice. From then on, the people of the small town would talk about the blind child kneeling in front of the tabernacle almost every day, always murmuring something. In truth, she was unburdening herself.

"What would happen to me when I grow up? Dear Lord Jesus, I can't see!" she would pray. Children in her neighborhood and the men drinking on street corners were teasing her. "You're good for nothing, Dolor. You can't even see where you're walking!"

Then one day she met in her dreams a woman in a long white dress. "Poor girl, do not cry. Do you want to do something worthwhile?" the woman asked the blind girl.

Dolor said nothing.

"Help my other children. Don't be sad just because you cannot see," the woman said. Before Dolor could speak, the woman was gone.

She had another dream a few days later. This time she saw the bearded man. Blood was oozing from his shoulders. Wounds covered his body.

"Look at me," the wounded man said.

"Who are you? How could I look at you, sir? I am blind," Dolor replied.

"Just do what I tell you. Look at me and you will see," the man said. In her dream, Dolor raised her head and looked up.

"Help me heal my wounds," the man said. "I have been in pain for a very long time. My wounds have never healed. Help me, my little blind girl."

"How can I help you? I don't know anything." She could not move, but she could not look away either.

"You can heal me. Believe in God, believe in yourself, and do what you can," the man said. He then told Dolor that he would give her a gift. "Every time you help other people, especially the sick, I will be healed and my wounds will go away."

"You will look at people's palms and know what others have a hard time knowing. But never tell the people about what will happen. Instead of making them afraid, let them experience love and care," the man continued.

He warned Dolor not to tell pregnant women if their child were a boy or a girl. "It is enough that you will know," the bearded man said. "And never forget to fast on Fridays and during Holy Week," he instructed. "Pray for the people so that my wounds would heal and the blood would stop."

One evening, when only the croaking of the frogs in the field could be heard, the bearded man came back to visit Dolor. He taught her how to knead people's muscles and massage the pain away. After almost an hour, the man was gone and Dolor woke up into another dark day.

Even at thirteen, she knew it was God she saw in her dreams. But she never tried the gift of healing the man said he had entrusted to her. "It was just a dream," she would say.

By the time she turned nineteen, however, she had become unbearably curious about the gift. She continued to go to church, but nothing seemed to have changed in her life. When she remembered what the bearded man once taught her, she thought of trying it out on some friends.

She applied coconut oil on Lourdes Alojado one day when the woman complained of body pains and was running a high fever. The next day Lourdes claimed she got well because of Dolor. From then on, Lourdes became Dolor's constant companion and friend.

The blind woman did not tell her family and other friends what she was capable of doing. She made it a point to help only those who would ask for her help, or those she believed had already suffered a long time.

Then the bearded man came back after several years of absence. "Now that you believe, you must help the poor," he said.

She gave up everything to do just that. Despite surrendering herself to serve others, however, her own life became filled with sacrifice and pain. Maybe it was already written on her palm, some said.

She was born to a mestiza Chinese mother and a mestizo Waray father. She had a sister and a brother by her first father. Her beautiful mother sold goods around town to support the family. The day came, however, when trading did not appeal to her anymore. She fell in love with another man and left Dolor's father.

Her mother brought her along to her new father. At first she was glad that she could be with her mother, until she realized her new home was a living hell. Her mother became irritable and was always angry. His stepfather, a Muslim, sometimes hurt her. They did not want her, the blind one, to go to church. They wanted her to stay in the house and take care of her step-brothers and stepsisters.

She endured until the day she could have a family of her own. But Dolor's own marriage was no escape from pain. She didn't even know the man she married.

One Sunday morning, while walking to church, a man told Dolor he had a mestizo Muslim-Chinese friend who wanted to marry her. "One of these days, you will become his wife," the man said.

"I don't want to get married. I want to be a nun," the beautiful blind young lady said. "Anyway, how do you know that I will marry him when I don't even know the man?"

A few months after that conversation, on May 16, 1981, the man who walked Dolor to church raped her inside her own room, inside her own hut, somewhere in the war-torn town of Isabela.

"He tied my neck and my arms with towels. He covered my mouth. Then I felt the pain. It was indescribable," Dolor would later tell her friend, Basilan Bishop Querexeta, the young Spanish priest who once told her to talk to Jesus in the tabernacle.

"You are an animal," the bishop shouted at the man. "Why did you do it to this blind girl? You did not even have pity."

"She liked me," the man reasoned.

"You will rot in jail," Bishop Querexeta said.

"Then I will leave for the mountains to join the rebels," the man answered.

"You can go to hell," the bishop said.

The man later offered to marry Dolor. They got married on November 18, 1981, but the marriage did not last long. On January 9, 1992, the husband was found dead.

Dolor believed her husband was killed because he had become a Christian. His family and their friends and relatives were angry with him for marrying Dolor. They said, Not only did you marry a Christian, you married a blind Christian!

As a Muslim or as a Christian, however, Dolor's husband did not change his ways. Dolor would later say: "No matter how much one promises to be better, one can still be bad."

She said her husband would bring other women to their house, even ordering her to cook for them. In the evening, the other woman would share their bed, Dolor playing deaf to the moaning and grinding beside her.

One day she talked to her husband's companion of the moment.

"What day do you go to church?" Dolor asked her.

"On Wednesdays," the girl answered.

"Wednesday is the day of the Mother of Perpetual Help," Dolor said. "If you really believe in God and have faith in him, why do you go with a person who already has a wife who is even blind?"

"If you won't leave my husband, you will forever live in sin. Your prayers will have no effect," Dolor warned.

After a week, the woman left for the Visayas, leaving Dolor's husband behind. Four months later, he was killed.

"People become bad because they always want more in life. They are not content with what they have. If only people will help other people, then there would be peace," Dolor would tell her patients every time they ask for her counsel.

When asked one time why she didn't simply leave the island to live a new life in some other land, Dolor said: "I don't want to leave Basilan because it was here where I learned about life."

Maybe it was this simplicity of the innocent, coupled with a giggling laugh that reminded one of a child, that endeared Dolor to the Spanish bishop.

Before leaving for Spain in the twilight of his life, Bishop Querexeta left the blind woman a house and thousands of pesos in a bank. Old women whispered about it in church before praying the rosary at dusk. "The cash could last her two lifetimes!"

THE NEXT DAY, March 18, Dolor continued to attend to the people in Tumahubong; they grew in number starting at six in the morning. It was about the time when *gomeros* leave their homes to work at the rubber plantation. Dolor did not rest until the next morning, when she finished her session at one o'clock, Sunday morning.

She did not seem to have gotten tired. In answer to the many who asked, she told her patients that she was inspired by Father Rhoel's dedication. She stopped ministering only when the oil in the house, including the one for cooking, was all used up.

She rested for three hours. At four o'clock on Sunday morning, she started again and finished around five-thirty in the morning. At six-thirty, she was ready to go back to Isabela.

Before the sun rose high on the horizon, Dolor started walking toward the part of the village where the trucks waited for passengers. On her way, an old woman touched Dolor on the shoulder. "Don't go. Do not leave," the woman said.

"I know," Dolor answered, as if she knew that someone would stop her along the way. "Something will happen. I'm expecting it."

"Then don't leave. Go on Monday. Tomorrow," the woman tried again.

"No, I'm sorry. It is good for me to leave now. It is better that I go," Dolor said.

The woman led Dolor toward the waiting truck. With a stick in her right hand, Dolor had to struggle to walk on the muddy road. She heard the tolling of the broken church bell. Father Rhoel must be busy now preparing for Mass, she thought. She could smell the aroma of the pine trees with the protruding roots.

Then she felt it. Something was in the air.

"*Manang* Dolor, *Manang* Dolor," someone called her name. She stopped. The old woman who was holding her left arm was gone.

"Wait for me, *Manang*. I'll go with you." She recognized the voice. It was 22-year-old Marissa Rante, the teacher who lived just across the street from the chapel. Marissa was Father Rhoel's best friend.

"Marie, can you feel it?" Dolor asked Marissa, who now walked beside her, holding on to her arm.

"What, *Manang*?"

"I feel different. I feel something will happen," Dolor answered.

"*Buyag, Manang*! I'm still coming back this afternoon," Marissa said. She was going to Isabela to pick up the pins and medals the Claret School of Tumahubong would use for the graduation rites the following week.

"Something is in the air. Something hard to explain," Dolor said. "The air is not cold but it is different."

It was a familiar feeling, like the many times she knew it would rain, or she knew there would be an accident, or she knew somebody would die the following day.

It was the same feeling she had on that fateful Valentine's Day. Days before the incident, Dolor chanced upon *Manong* Emiliano, the trusted old driver of the priests and missionaries. He had served the church for many years, even before most priests on the island had entered the seminary.

Nong Emiliano always traveled at dawn, and that day Dolor warned him to take care of himself. "You're old now, *Manong*. Don't be too eager to leave early in the morning. You know the bandits are always around," she said.

But the old man dismissed the blind woman's reminder. "All the rebels and bandits in this island know me, Dolor. I got old in these dangerous areas. And you know, only God knows what will happen. And he will take care of me."

"Shhh, *Manong*. There are people out to betray you. They might even use a bolo on you," Dolor said.

"Only God knows," the old man said with finality.

Just before Dolor left the convent, Father Rhoel caught up with her.

"Before you go, you must also look at my hand," he said in jest. Dolor obliged.

Her face turned white, then her lips trembled. The priest thought it was because she did not have enough sleep.

"Be careful, Father. I see the sign on your palm. You have it, too. It is written there. This must be something big," Dolor said.

"Shhh, Dolor. Don't worry. If they take me, then I will go with them. But I will fight back," the priest said, laughing.

"If you fight back, they will kill you. There will be many of them and you are alone," Dolor said.

The priest turned serious and composed himself. "It was just a joke, Dolor. A bad joke," he said. "Please, pray for me."

It was Sunday, March 19.

CHAPTER 2

THE FOG WAS A CURTAIN that refused to part the day the bandits came. The dew that gathered on the leaves did not drop. Even the birds refused to fly. Something ominous was hovering over the lethargic little village of Tumahubong.

THE MORNING THE BANDITS CAME

Angelita Grado, or Angie to friends and co-workers at Claret School, woke up at 5:30 that morning. For one who lives in a village where people get up at 4:30 am to prepare for work in the rubber plantation, this was seriously late. (In her village, electricity is turned on at that exact time to let the *gomeros*, the men and women who collect the sap of rubber trees, prepare their tools. An hour later the electricity is turned off.)

"*Gitapol ko adtong adlawa. Bug-at kaayo akong lawas ug wala koy gana moadto sa eskwelahan* (I felt lazy that day. My body was heavy and I didn't want to go to school)," Angie would tell her friends later. She did not know why but she felt that that particular Monday morning was different. The previous night, she had dreamt of people dying. She dreamt of her mother, who was killed by bandits the previous year.

If you don't feel too good, her aunt said, why don't you just stay in the house? But it was Monday, March 20, the first day of the last week of school. Angie, the school cashier, knew she had to go to work.

She hurried to the back of the house. The water in the plastic bucket was freezing. She took a cold bath as fast as she could.

After putting on her uniform of peach blouse and blue skirt, Angie walked to school without eating breakfast. I will eat after the flag ceremony, she told herself. The school was less than a kilometer away from her house.

Ahead of her, she saw Analyn Pascua and Anabelle Mendoza also walking to school, studiously avoiding the potholes in the street. Both were teachers at Claret; both were her neighbors. Walking fast, Angie caught up with the two. "I had a dream last night," she told her two friends, breathlessly. "I saw a lot of dead people."

"Maybe the bandits will finally come and get us," Analyn joked. "Did you bring extra clothes with you?" she teased Angie.

For several months, the village had been absorbed in rumors that the Abu Sayyaf was out to kidnap teachers in the island. Just the previous Friday, March 17, Mr. Reynaldo Rubio, the school principal, received a letter from the bandits demanding P200 a month from each teacher. The school administration was also asked to give P10,000 a month.

The teachers and administrators held a meeting that afternoon, and decided not to give in to the bandits' demands. "Our salaries are not even enough to feed our families. How dare they make this demand on us? If they want to kill us, then let them come," one of the teachers said during the meeting.

When word of the teachers' refusal spread, rumors circulated that, this time, the bandits would surely come. A plantation worker warned Angie to be extra careful, but she just laughed the warnings off.

"We have been waiting for them for too long, but they have not come. *Ay Hesus*, we have been waiting for our Prince Charming. When are they coming?" Angie joked.

Anabelle, too, had a dream the previous night. "There will be war," she told Angie and Analyn as they were about to enter through the school gate.

"How come we had the same dream?" Angie replied. "Maybe you're making fun of me!" She turned to Analyn, who was smiling. "Don't tell me you also had a dream last night?"

"Yes, I also had the same dream," Analyn admitted. "Remember what happened on March 10? We had a seminar at the parish convent when the Philippine flag in front of the school building fell. It was a bad omen, *hala*."

The three laughed.

"Let's promise each other," Angie said. "If there will be war, let us survive. In war, some die, others survive. Let us make sure that we will be the ones to survive."

The friends agreed.

They passed the rusty gate and proceeded to the school grounds in front of the flagpole. The students were already there, lining up for the flag ceremony. At the nearby public elementary school, the children were already singing the national anthem.

It was a few minutes past seven in the morning.

TUMAHUBONG IS A FORBIDDING PLACE. Even without the rumors that bandits are camped near the village, residents of nearby areas refuse to visit because of the rugged road the women have dubbed "Abortion Highway." (The name, with typical Filipino humor, suggests that the road will not be kind to pregnant women.)

The village sits on one side of Basilan's mountainous terrain facing the island province of Sulu. From the provincial capital of Isabela, a visitor has to endure a grueling four-hour jeep or truck ride through the towns of Lamitan and Tipo-Tipo.

There are huge boulders in the middle of the one-lane road, sometimes alternating with the deep potholes filled with the previous night's rain.

Wild hagonoy and cogon grasses line either side of the road; these have camouflaged bandits and rebels roaming the area many times in the past. Along the winding highway reside the Yakans, a tribe indigenous to Basilan. Most of them have embraced Islam and are called Moros. They live in thatched houses made of wood, bamboo, cogon, nipa, or anahaw leaves.

In the town of Tipo-Tipo is a marketplace where people sell or barter fish and vegetables on Wednesdays. Not far from the market is a *langgal* or small mosque with a graceful dome topped by the star and crescent. Muslims in the community come here to worship, especially on Fridays.

As the road leads closer to Tumahubong, the traveler can see the forest. It is there, people say, where the bandits are living with the wild animals.

The tortuous road that passes through Tipo-Tipo ends in the small village of Tumahubong, where the laughter and giggling of children greet newcomers. Tumahubong is one of 41 villages in the town of Sumisip. The place is predominantly Christian, although Muslims, mostly belonging to the Yakan tribe, also live there.

At the center of the village is the San Vicente Ferrer Parish church. Inside the church is a statue of the patron saint, believed by most Catholics in the village to be miraculous. Many times in the past, bandits attacked the village and tried to destroy the statue, but today it remains intact.

In front of the church is a grassy lot where children play. Not far from the church is the government-run elementary school. Beside it is the Claret High School of Tumahubong, established by the Claretian priests. The school caters mostly to Muslim children from nearby villages.

Early every morning, students in their checkered uniforms are a sight to see when they walk to school. Those from other villages would be lugging their lunch, packed in banana leaves or plastic bags.

Near the school is the village market where Muslim women sell fish, vegetables, fruits, and chicken. The camp of the Philippine Army's 10th Infantry Battalion is just a few meters away.

ANGIE WENT UP STRAIGHT to the Faculty Room where she found Mr. Rubio and Father Rhoel Gallardo inside their cubicles. What is Father doing here? she thought. It was a Monday and it was supposed to be his day off.

"Good morning," the priest greeted Angie.

"Good morning, Father," the teacher answered. "What happened to you, Father? Are you sick? You're not supposed to be here," Angie teased the priest. "And look at you," she added, pointing to Father Rhoel's hair. "As if you're preparing for your wake. You're all dressed up," she said.

"I just feel good," Father Rhoel replied, smiling.

Angie opened a desk drawer as the priest went outside to greet the teachers who were on their way to their classrooms. Angie could hear the priest and the teachers laughing. "He's in high spirits today. What happened to him, Sir?" Angie asked Mr. Rubio.

"I don't know. I was surprised too," the principal said. "I was preparing for another quarrel, but he was so warm and happy today."

Almost every morning, Father Rhoel and Mr. Rubio had arguments over how to run the school.

"He's back," Angie whispered to Mr. Rubio when she saw the priest returning to the room. She started counting the medals on her table.

"Are you going to Isabela today, Father?" she asked. "We need more medals for the graduates."

"Yes. I'm leaving immediately."

Mr. Rubio listened to them while checking some examination papers. He wanted to appear busy. He did not want to join the conversation. He was afraid that Father Rhoel would again argue with him about something.

"Father, can I have breakfast first before I finish this?" Angie asked the priest.

"No, I'm about to leave. You eat later. Anyway you will not die if you do not eat now," Father Rhoel said, laughing.

The two went over the list of honor students in silence.

"Sir, look here," Angie called on Mr. Rubio. She knew that the school principal and the priest were not at ease with each other. She wanted them to talk.

"These are our plans for the graduation," Angie approached Mr. Rubio. The priest followed her inside the school principal's cubicle.

MANANG INTANG SALBURO was tending to her vegetable garden beside the elementary school when she heard a loud explosion. She instinctively dropped to the ground and did not move. What followed was an experience that she will never forget.

"It seemed like forever," she recalled. "The gunfire, the explosions, it was like the end of the world. I just prayed. What more can I do? What more can a Christian do in times of fear?"

Finally, the old woman heard the explosions stop. There was only sporadic gunfire now. She crawled back to her house, a few meters away from the school. She looked for her grandchildren, all grade school students. She called for them, but they were not there.

She ran outside, not minding the gunfire anymore. She ran toward the school. But armed men blocked her way. "Old woman, go back," a teenager in a black long-sleeved shirt shouted. He was carrying a rifle.

"Kill me if you want, just give me back the children," she cried.

KIPYONG GREGORIO, an18-year-old who behaves like a child half his age, woke up late for his Grade Four class. "I woke up late because I live near the school," he said later.

When he heard the national anthem winding down, Kipyong sneaked into the school through a gap in the barbed wire fence. He meant to avoid the teachers looking out for late students.

Then he saw the armed men approach the school from the back. The boy was excited. He watched the men who were all in black—boots, pants, sweatshirts, bonnets—stealthily approach the school. Kipyong watched them in awe. He was always impressed with how soldiers carry themselves. They look handsome in their uniforms.

Then he saw a flash of light come out from the tip of one of the long guns a man was carrying on his shoulder. A deafening explosion followed. Kipyong ran for his life toward his classroom.

ANGIE WAS THE FIRST in Claret to see the men in black.

The school was already silent. The teachers and students were already in their rooms. Classes had already started. Angie glanced at the clock on the wall. It was 7:49. One more hour and it would be recess time, and then she could finally eat her breakfast.

Angie looked outside the window. It was a cloudy day. She saw that the cogon grass at the back of the building had grown taller. Time to ask the students to trim it again, she thought.

Then she saw the men. They were in black and all of them were wearing red scarves on their heads. Some were wearing black sweatshirts with "Army 2000" printed in front. Others were in military uniforms. All were carrying assorted firearms, the sort of weapons Angie saw only the Army's Special Forces carry around. There was also a bazooka.

Just like in the movies, she thought.

"Sir. Rebels," Angie whispered to Mr. Rubio. Then they heard the blast. Angie was stunned. She could not move. Then another blast. And then another.

MR. RUBIO LOOKED OUTSIDE the window. He could sense Father Rhoel moving behind him, peeping through the wooden jalousies.

Seeing the men, the priest sprung and rushed outside, past Angie's table, through the left door of the Faculty Room, toward the left wing of the building. It became clear that what he wanted to do was to close the iron gate of the second floor.

He was about to lock the gate when bandits appeared before him on the other side of the iron grill. They were pointing their guns at him. The priest raised his arms. They approached him and held him tight. From behind, somebody hit Father Rhoel with the butt of a rifle.

"Come down, fast," the men shouted at the priest. They thought Father Rhoel was a teacher. They brought him downstairs, in front of the building where a few minutes ago the children sang the national anthem. They had a piece of rope with them, which they used to tie the priest's arms.

Mr. Rubio went to the right door of the Faculty Room, toward the middle entrance of the second floor. "Close the doors," he shouted at the top of his voice. The gunfire drowned his orders. He could hear the students shouting and crying. The rebels were already downstairs. He could hear their boots pounding the concrete floor, coming toward him, climbing the stairs.

Then there was another deafening explosion. More students rushed upstairs. Mr. Rubio thought it was useless to go down. He followed the students back to the Faculty Room, in the middle of the second floor of the building. They closed the doors.

The bandits followed them. They banged on the doors of the Faculty Room. Mr. Rubio looked up. He remembered the ceiling. There they would be safe. There was a manhole near the right door that would lead him up the ceiling to the roof of the building. They had practiced climbing it in the past in preparation for this kind of emergency. But everything seemed useless now. There were too many of them in the room and the bandits were already at the door. There was no time.

He motioned the students to move to one corner where he believed they would be safe if the bandits started shooting from outside. He remembered his .45 caliber pistol inside his drawer. He crawled to his desk and took it. For a few seconds he thought of fighting it out. But there were too many of them, he thought. It would be useless. He threw the gun into the thrash bin and covered it with crumpled papers.

The bandits kicked the door open. The children inside the room, at least 15 of them, were already crying. The bandits entered. Mr. Rubio raised his arms. One of the armed men approached him and snatched his wristwatch. Another bandit saw the national flag in one corner. He took the rope that held the flag to the pole and used it to tie the arms of the school principal. They also tied one of the teachers, Wenifer Silorio, who was eight months pregnant.

The bandits shooed the students outside the room and dragged the teachers downstairs. Mr. Rubio saw Father Rhoel already on the school grounds, his arms bound. The priest was pleading with the bandits not to bring Marissa Rante because she was sick and Wenifer because she was pregnant.

"Don't lecture us," one bandit shouted at the priest. "You are our prisoners."

THERE WERE TWO GROUPS of bandits who attacked Tumahubong that morning. The group headed by Abu Sabaya, the group's spokesman, went to the elementary school while the one headed by Khaddafy Janjalani, the group's leader, entered Claret School.

"It was really just like in the movies," Angie would later say.

There were snipers all around the village. In case soldiers stationed a few meters away moved on them, the bandits would have used the students and teachers as a shield.

The situation was tense, but some students found an element of fun in it. The girls said most of the bandits were good-looking. One student later told Angie: "Ma'am, they are really handsome, especially the one who came looking for you."

"Why didn't you tell me? I could have come out from my hiding place and went with them. What a pity," Angie replied in kind, laughing.

Many of the bandits were teenagers. The older ones were in their twenties. They were just kids, Mr. Rubio thought. But they were still dangerous, because they were armed and very aggressive. The younger ones were all eager to kill. When they came, they just started shooting. They concentrated their fire on the military camp near the school.

THE FIRST BLAST of the big gun stunned Angie. She was not able to move. The second explosion, however, startled her into action. While Father Rhoel rushed outside to close the gate of the second floor and Mr. Rubio shouted at the students to close the doors, Angie was already safe under her desk in front of the left door of the Faculty Room.

"*Mamang*, I will die now," she silently called on the spirit of her dead mother, trembling. "Lord, if I will die, please forgive my sins." She crouched lower under the table.

Who are these men? Are they the Abu Sayyaf? Or are they plain bandits? Angie remembered the drill they had followed in the past, which involved climbing up the ceiling. She used to joke that because she could not climb the ceiling, she would just hide under the table if the bandits came.

Gloria Elman, a colleague of Angie's, told her then, "If you do that, I will tell the bandits where you are."

But that joke prepared Angie; it told her what to do. Gloria was also able to hide under her table, thanks to Angie's simple idea.

Angie heard the armed men kick the door open, the one where Mr. Rubio went through. A bandit shouted at the students: "Are you Muslims or Christians?" The students shouted back, saying they were Muslims. "Then go downstairs, you are free," the bandit ordered the children. They scampered down; all of them were Christians.

Then Angie heard someone trying to open the door in front of her table. It was locked. Then she heard the window grills shot at. Finally someone opened the door for the man, who immediately entered the room and stood beside the table where Angie was hiding. She saw blood dripping on the floor, a few inches from her. "The man must be hurt," Angie thought.

WENIFER WAS IN THE CLASSROOM with her students when she heard the explosion and the ensuing gunfire. She went on with her class, thinking it was just another military exercise.

When one of the bandits entered the room, Wenifer thought the man was a soldier. "Who is the teacher here?" the man asked respectfully.

"I am," Wenifer volunteered. "What can I do for you, Sir?"

"Ma'am, can you come with me? I just want to talk to you about something," the man said. Wenifer followed the man who held her lightly on the elbow. "This soldier is a gentleman," she thought.

It was only when they entered the Faculty Room that reality hit Wenifer. She saw Mr. Rubio's arms already tied. "Sir; what happened here?" she asked the school principal. Mr. Rubio did not answer. "What is this, Sir? Kidnapping?" By now Wenifer was trembling.

"We will go with you, but please don't bring the pregnant woman," she heard Mr. Rubio pleading.

"We don't care. We don't care if she will die on the way," one of the bandits answered.

"Animals!" Angie cursed from her hiding place.

When they were downstairs, Father Rhoel also pleaded with the bandits not to bring Wenifer. He asked the armed men to spare the students. Instead, the bandits pointed their guns at the children and threatened to shoot.

The priest dropped to his knees, pleading. "Spare the children. If you are looking for me, I will go. I am a priest. But don't bring the children," Father Rhoel said. He was already crying. "Please have pity on the pregnant teacher. We will go with you. We will not leave you until you get the money that you want, just leave the teacher."

A bandit approached the kneeling priest from behind and hit him on the back with the butt of a rifle.

Angie heard everything from her hiding place. She wanted to come out and volunteer herself if only the bandits would leave the pregnant Wenifer behind. "I really planned to come out if the bandits said they would leave Wenifer if somebody volunteered to take her place. But when I heard that they had decided to bring Wenifer, I decided to continue hiding. Are they crazy? I was not going with them."

FEMALE STUDENTS HID MARISSA, who is just four feet and a few inches tall, under their skirts when the bandits came. But when the armed men ordered the students to get out, the children scampered toward the door, leaving the small teacher in the middle of the abandoned classroom.

People later joked that Marissa was found out because she could not stand the smell of her students' underwear.

JOY REAMBONANZA, another teacher, was joking with friends on her way to school that morning. She said she was bringing extra food that day in preparation for the coming of the kidnappers. She had no idea that at the very moment her joke was coming true.

Her three children went to school ahead of her. Joy was still preparing her things when the children said goodbye. She told them to go ahead. At around 7:15, she passed by the elementary school on her way to Claret and gave the children money for their snacks.

Joy saw the rebels through the window of her first-floor classroom as she was about to start her class that morning. The students saw them too. "Ma'am, look! Rebels!"

"Help me, please. Those are Abu Sayyaf, hide me from them," she asked her students. She wanted to run to the second floor to hide inside the Faculty Room, but she heard the armed men coming. There was no more time to get out of the room. I am going to die now, she thought.

"Father, we will be together already because I will die soon," she called on her dead father. She started to pray the Our Father.

More explosions tore the air. She could hear the gunshots coming nearer.

One of her students then pushed her to the floor. Someone sat on her back. Then another followed. She could feel at least four students sitting on her. Then the others, all 53 of them, sat around her in the center of the room.

"Pray," she told them.

"God is great, Allah is merciful," the students started reciting a Muslim prayer. Joy had only three Christian students. The rest were all Muslims.

"Open the door," the bandits shouted from outside.

"We will not open the door. You already got our teacher. We will not allow you to get us," the students shouted back.

"Where is your teacher?" a bandit shouted.

"She's upstairs," the students answered as they continued praying.

The bandits left. Joy waited. The students continued praying. All of them had tears in their eyes. Some of the girls were weeping. But they continued to pray amid their sobbing. After what seemed like an eternity, there was silence. Joy stood up, opened the door, and ran outside. The students ran with her, covering her escape.

"Ma'am, if the rebels will take you, we will come with you," one of them said. Joy was not able to hold her tears. She cried and thanked all of them. They all ran faster. Joy took off her uniform's blazer and threw it away. They ran outside the school grounds to a nearby house where someone gave her a change of clothes. She was already trembling.

Then she remembered her three children. She ran to the elementary school with her students. The children were not there. She shouted their names. Nobody answered. She ran toward the church, to the convent, leaving her students behind. She thought of calling the bishop in Isabela to tell him about the bandits, but she did not know how to operate the trunk radio.

WHEN ANGIE COULD NO LONGER HEAR ANYTHING from under her table, she came out slowly. Seeing that the armed men were no longer around, she ran downstairs, looked around, and then ran again toward the nearest gate. Her dress caught on the barbed wire fence. She took her dress off and ran in her underwear outside the school compound. She did not know where to go, but she just felt the need to run, not wanting to stop. She stopped only when she fell into a shallow ravine.

She heard people laughing. When she looked up, some students were smiling at her. One Muslim boy took off his shirt and gave it to Angie. It was then that she realized she was practically naked. A good thing I was wearing my new bra, she said later. Then she started crying. She looked for her companions, and found Joy and Gloria. They were safe.

But Father Rhoel, Mr. Rubio, Wenifer, Marissa, Anabelle, and some children were gone.

"Let us go to church," Angie said. There was chaos. People were shouting and running around. The teachers ran toward the church, then to the convent. Using Father Rhoel's two-way radio, they called the Claretians in nearby Maluso town and informed them of the kidnapping.

"Let us pray," Angie, who was also a catechist, said. "Let us show them that despite what happened, we are not going to lose our faith. Let us show them that Christians are not afraid."

So they went to church and prayed the rosary. They also read the Bible.

Then the parents of the abducted children came crying. "Ma'am, we don't know what to do," they said.

"Let us all pray. Let us get our strength from Him," Angie said. She didn't know how, but she found herself giving a little speech. "We have to accept the fact that life is like that, some have to leave while others are left behind. But let us not show to these bandits that by taking our priest and our children we will lose our faith. Let us show them that we are strong." As she was talking she started to cry again.

After the prayers, the teachers comforted those who were crying. They shared funny anecdotes about the attack to lighten the moment. "We had to do it," Angie would later say. "If we didn't do it, nothing would have happened and the whole village would surrender to the bandits," she added.

"People here depend on the church for strength. When they took our priest, we had to stand on our own and had to be strong," Angie said.

WHEN THE ABU SAYYAF LEFT with their hostages, *Manang* Intang followed them. Along the road she pleaded for the release of her grandchildren. The bandits shooed her back, but she kept on walking, following them from a distance.

"I have nothing to lose. I am old already and the children are still young. If I die, then I die, but I have to get the children." *Manang* Intang was alone, but she was not afraid. She knew the area. She had worked in the plantation for three decades.

After several kilometers, the bandits pointed their guns at the old woman. *Manang* Intang thought it was useless. She went back to the village. Along the way she met a Muslim woman who was also looking for her child. They decided to walk together and follow the bandits through another route. But they could not find them anymore.

AFTER PRAYING WITH ANGIE, Joy went back to the elementary school to look for her children. Some students said the bandits took all her three kids. The first thing that came to Joy's mind was her smallest daughter. She's too small and she's not used to walking. She fought back tears. "Let's come up with a plan," she told the other parents who were congregating at the school grounds. Everybody was crying.

ON THEIR WAY to the mountains, the bandits asked the children who among them were Muslims. One elementary student said she was. The Abu Sayyaf told her to go home. But the girl refused. "Not without these three small children," she said, pointing to Joy's children. "I will stay, just release them," the Muslim girl said.

"But they are Christians," a bandit argued.

"They are my neighbors too," said the Muslim girl.

"We will let the youngest girl go with you," the bandits said. "Go home," they told the two girls. On their way back to the village, however, Joy's daughter kept crying. She wanted to be with her brothers. So the two decided to go back and join the bandits.

"Why are you coming back?" the Abu Sayyaf asked.

"The young girl wants to be with her brothers," the Muslim girl said.

Eventually, all four of them were released after three days in the mountains. When they got back, the first thing the small girl told her mother was: "Mama, not all Muslims are bad. They are also like us."

But while confusion reigned in the village, a group of Christians living near the school ransacked the abandoned building and took off with some of the kidnapped teachers' personal things, including a camera, several wallets, and even signing pens.

Said a Muslim who later learned of the incident, "Not all Christians are good too."

IT WAS ALREADY AROUND FIVE O'CLOCK in the afternoon when the bandits and their hostages reached camp. It was only then, after the sun had set, that the bandits introduced themselves to their hostages.

THE BEARER OF THE SWORD

AHMAD SAMPANG is a 26-year-old Tausug. He was the *amir* or leader of the urban hit squad of the Abu Sayyaf in Basilan from June 1992 to December 1998.

He was just 17 years old when he joined the Abu Sayyaf. He was one of the "pioneers" of the group formed by Ustadz Abdurajak Abubakar Janjalani, a young idealistic Muslim preacher who studied Islam in the Middle East.

There were at least 30 of them.

Among the original members of the group were Abdurajak's brother Hector Janjalani, now under arrest; Edwin Angeles, a.k.a. Yusuf Ibrahim, later discovered to be a government military asset, now dead; and Muhamad Wahab Akbar, the recently reelected governor of Basilan province.

The other pioneers were young Muslim students from the towns of Isabela, Lamitan, Maluso, Lantawan, and Sumisip, all in the province of Basilan.

Sampang (a pseudonym he assumed after "escaping" the Abu Sayyaf) was a computer engineering student at A.E. Colleges in Zamboanga City when he was invited to join the group. He was told that the Muslim *Ummah* or community needed people to assert the teachings of the Qur'an.

Sampang was a friend of Hector's, and his classmate in a *madrasah* [Islamic school] where Abdurajak preached every Friday.

"*Nakumbinse kami sa mga itinuro niya sa amin tungkol sa Islam* (We were persuaded by what [Abdurajak] taught us about Islam)," Sampang recalls. "Christians laugh at us, oppress and despise us." The only way to get back at Christians, Abdurajak said, was through a jihad, a holy war.

Fired up by Abdurajak's ideas, the student-pioneers were sent to nearby Sulu province for clandestine military training.

"We went there as students. We bought our student identification cards for P20 at the Basilan National High School," Sampang says. To get a boat ride to Jolo, the capital of Sulu, they had to pass through busy Zamboanga City.

In order not to arouse suspicion, the young recruits were told to bring only an extra pair of pants, three T-shirts, and some high school textbooks.

"I can still remember that I brought with me a book about Jose Rizal with the Philippine flag on its cover," Sampang says.

When the soldiers manning the port asked them for identification, the recruits said they were students going home to Jolo for the weekend.

Their destination was the Abu Sayyaf training camp in the village of Tugas, in Patikul town in Sulu. It was just a stone's throw away from a military detachment.

"We even got water from where the soldiers got theirs," Sampang says. "When they asked us who we were, we said we were students out camping at a nearby village."

The soldiers actually visited the camping site, but they found nothing incriminating. The firearms were well hidden, Sampang says. And the four foreign trainers—three Afghans and a Syrian—hid easily in the nearby trees.

"It was hard during the basic training. It took us two weeks. But after that, we were used to the routine," Sampang says.

"We woke up at 4:30 in the morning for prayers, then we jogged and did calisthenics. We crawled, rolled, and did physical exercises."

After breakfast, at around 9 a.m., they were taught the use and maintenance of firearms.

At 11:30 a.m., they ate and rested.

At midday they recited the noon prayers together, after which they studied the Qur'an.

At 3:30 p.m. they prayed together again. Then after that, more physical exercises and combat training.

It was in Tugas where Sampang learned to use the M-16, the M-14, the 90RR, the 57RR, the 60mm mortar, the M203.

After three months of training, the group went back to Basilan.

Sampang was assigned to head the group's "urban demolition squad" based in Isabela, the provincial capital. His unit's assignment: assassinate soldiers and people who refused to give money.

He will not say how many he killed, only that, when he sensed that the finger of suspicion was pointed at him, he joined his comrades in the mountains, in the village of Makiri, in the town of Lantawan.

THEY CALLED THEMSELVES the Al-Harakatul Islamia; by some twist, however, their group became better known as the Abu Sayyaf or "Father of the Sword"—a reference to Abdurajak, the group's founder and ideologue.

The phrase, however, was mistranslated by journalists and the military to "Bearer of the Sword."

"We grew in number because the people sympathized with us," Sampang says. "Whenever the military went on operations, they would harass ordinary civilians in rural areas. They would kill ordinary people, so the families of the victims joined us. A lot of people wanted to join the Abu Sayyaf then."

"People were supportive of us because when we got ransom money from the kidnappings, we gave them money. When they asked for pump boats [motorized outriggers], we gave them. We gave it to them for their livelihood."

In Lantawan, he says, people were very supportive of the Abu Sayyaf. "They would hide our firearms. That is why the military could not catch us or follow us."

In exchange, they gave the people animals for livelihood projects, such as goats and chicken for raising. "If a landlord would threaten tenants, we would kill the landlord, [whether it was] day or night."

They didn't kill indiscriminately, he adds quickly. "We do our thing in an organized manner."

This was the reason, he says, that they were able to convince a lot of people to support them.

Once, he says, they were able to reduce electricity and water rates in the province after they sent a letter to the managers of the local electric company and the water district.

"We told them that the poor could not avail themselves of electricity and water because of the high rates."

"We warned the company that if they did not lower the rates, the Abu Sayyaf would sabotage their operations." Sampang says the strategy was Abdurajak's idea. Abdurajak, he says, wanted "to help those who were oppressed."

Like Osama bin Ladin, the terrorist who declared war on the United States, Abdurajak was a veteran of the war in Afghanistan. But Abdurajak did not teach his followers to be angry with Christians, Sampang says.

"We were angry with government leaders. We didn't like how they were running our country. During Christian holy days there are no classes, but on Muslim holy days, Muslims have to go to school or work."

"The idea of Abdurajak was for Muslims and Christians in Mindanao to work together. We respect their freedom of religion. What we wanted is for us, Muslims, to freely practice the teachings of the Qur'an and for Christians to respect it."

Abdurajak was not able to match his rhetoric with deeds, however. He was lured by quick military successes and easy money. He approved the kidnapping spree of Christians that went on from 1992 to 1994.

When he died in December 1998, in a firefight with the police in a village on the border of Isabela and Lamitan, his group appeared to have finally lost its political ideals.

Sampang remembers that on the day Abdurajak was killed, there were only seven of them hiding in a safe house, and that Abdurajak had instructed him to go to the capital town that morning to buy supplies.

"I only learned later that evening that there had been an encounter in the area where we were hiding. I learned the next day that my companions were killed."

The whole group was demoralized. "Abdurajak was a big loss. He was a good person. He knew how to handle people. He did not pressure anybody, unlike the other leaders."

After Abdurajak's death, a power struggle took place within the organization, with the former leader's younger brother, Khaddafy Janjalani, finally emerging as the new chief. Hector, the former military commander and Khaddafy's older brother, was by then in jail.

Khaddafy, a.k.a. Abu Mochtar, is "good-hearted," Sampang says. "The problem is he cannot make his own decisions. He needs advisers, unlike Abdurajak."

Under Khaddafy's leadership, the Abu Sayyaf became a kidnap-for-ransom gang with an extremist view of Islam. In his time, the group exploded in number. From around 650 members in the early 1990s, the Abu Sayyaf is now believed to have grown to almost 3,000 fighters.

But as their number grew, the violence they wrought on their targets also worsened. Despite the Abu Sayyaf's continued attacks on helpless civilians, however, Khaddafy enjoyed a reputation as a "kind-hearted" Abu Sayyaf.

Hostages kidnapped in Tumahubong in Basilan said that Khaddafy, unlike the group's spokesman Abu Sabaya, was kind.

"He was gentle and he would always give instructions to his men to take it easy with the kidnapped children," said a former kidnap victim.

A teacher who was hostaged by the bandits was thankful that "between two evils," it was Khaddafy who led the kidnapping in Claret High School and not the grim Abu Sabaya who led the raid on the nearby elementary school.

"Sabaya was more violent and harsh. Khaddafy was at least meek and kind to the hostages," the teacher recalled.

Another kidnap victim said Khaddafy was good-looking. "He did not look at all like he was a bandit," said a young female student who saw the long-haired Abu Sayyaf leader.

By the late 1990s, however, it was Abu Sabaya, the group's spokesman notorious for his threats aired over local radio stations, who became the public face of the Abu Sayyaf. During the Sipadan hostage crisis in 2000, he was joined by Ghalib Andang, alias Commander Robot, and Mujib Susukan, both former Moro National Liberation Front leaders in Sulu.

(During a major military operation against the Abu Sayyaf in Basilan in the mid-1990s, Abdurajak escaped to Sulu and sought refuge in the camps of Andang and Susukan. The charismatic preacher won the hearts of the two commanders, and convinced them to join the Abu Sayyaf as its leaders in Sulu.)

When Sampang heard Abu Sabaya in 2000 threatening Christians and urging Muslims to remove all the crosses in Basilan, he was discomfited.

"It is not right anymore," he says. "If only Abdurajak were still alive, he would not allow it. Innocent Muslims will be affected."

The original Abu Sayyaf got their money from kidnap-for-ransom operations. They also collected money from businessmen. "Most businessmen in the island would give us money and we would protect them," Sampang says.

In the early 1990s, the group asked P5,000 a month and several sacks of rice from each business establishment. "Sometimes they only gave us rice," Sampang says.

They also collected money from teachers and other professionals. "The teachers would give P50 a month."

When Abdurajak died, Khaddafy raised the demand to P200 a month from each teacher. "Of course people would give. They were afraid. How could they not be afraid when at least 50 fully armed men visited the schools?"

Some politicians also gave money to the group. "Governor Wahab Akbar supported us in the past. He was an original member, but he left after about two years because he did not become our leader."

The group, however, hated Congressman Abdulgani "Gerry" Salapuddin, a former MNLF commander.

"He did not help us. We asked him once to give us at least a few sacks of rice. But he failed us. We cannot kill him because he has a lot of armed men."

Abdurajak and his followers got most of their firearms from government soldiers. "We bought guns from them," says Sampang, who used to join what were called "retrieval operations."

A military six-by-six truck would motor to a pre-arranged point on the highway controlled by the bandits. The sol-

diers would then leave the cache of firearms on the roadside, covering it with coconut fronds and banana leaves. The
Abu Sayyaf would then retrieve the arms after the soldiers
left.

"Sometimes the soldiers would set us up," Sampang says.
"But we were always ready for it. We would be watching the
area for several days and if we knew that it was a set-up we
would not get the firearms for several days. There were always many of us when we collected the firearms, in case
there was a set-up."

The other guns, especially those used by the group of
Khaddafy, were bought from Malaysia. The big guns, however, those shown on television during the kidnapping of
the foreign tourists from Sipadan, were old pieces bought
from military camps in Zamboanga.

The Abu Sayyaf's activities include bombings, assassinations,
kidnappings, and extortion from companies and wealthy
businessmen.

The group's first major terrorist strike was a grenade attack
in 1991, in which two foreign women were killed. The following year, Abu Sayyaf militants hurled a bomb at a wharf
in the southern city of Zamboanga where the *MV Doulos,* an
international floating bookstore manned by Christian preachers, was docked. Several people were injured.

This attack was followed by similar bombings on the
Zamboanga airport and Roman Catholic churches. In 1993
the group bombed a cathedral in Davao City, killing seven
people.

The group has consistently targeted foreigners for kidnapping. In 1993, Abu Sayyaf gunmen kidnapped Charles
Walton, a language researcher for the Manila-based Sum-
mer Institute of Linguistics. Walton, then 61, was freed 23
days later.

The following year, the group kidnapped three Spanish nuns
and a Spanish priest in separate incidents.

In April 1995 the Abu Sayyaf carried out a vicious attack on the Christian town of Ipil in Zamboanga del Sur. Gunmen razed the town center to the ground and shot 53 civilians and soldiers dead. At that time, the military said the group had forged links with international terrorist cells.

In 1998, their victims included two Hong Kong men, a Malaysian, and a Taiwanese grandmother.

On April 23, 2000, a month after they took Father Rhoel Gallardo and his companions hostage, the Abu Sayyaf gained international notoriety when they raided a diving resort on Sipadan Island in Malaysia. In a lightning strike, they nabbed 21 mostly Western tourists and resort workers and took them back to their hideout in Sulu.

After the Sipadan kidnappings, the popularity of the Abu Sayyaf soared.

SAMPANG LEFT THE ABU SAYYAF in 1999.

"I left because the group lost its original reason for being. The activities were not anymore for Islam but for personal gratification. We abducted people not anymore for the cause of Islam but for money."

They got a lot of support from countries in the Middle East, especially during the early years of the organization. "Even our uniforms came from abroad. We were even issued bulletproof vests," he says.

In the past, however, they kidnapped people because they did not have funds to buy arms, bullets, and food. "There was a time when we didn't depend anymore on foreign funding. We were ashamed to continue asking for money from our sponsors abroad."

Sampang says that, even at that time, many of the original Abu Sayyaf members already wanted to surrender to the government. "But they were afraid that either the military would kill them or the group itself would hunt them down."

Sampang did not surrender. He says he just "escaped" from the group, changed his identity, and began working for a non-government organization.

His former comrades cannot harm him, he says.

"I am still armed and a lot of people I helped in the past are protecting me now."

Abu Sabaya's group went to his house once and tried to kill him. But Sampang was ready with his guns. "Allah protected me. I was able to escape."

Sampang said he does not like Abu Sabaya and the younger members of the group. "They behead dead soldiers and play with the bodies. They would swap the heads and cut the sex organs."

Sampang is not leaving Basilan, however.

"I was born here and I will die here."

CHAPTER 3

THE BANDITS DRAGGED THEIR CAPTIVES deep into the forest. From morning until late in the afternoon, they trudged on muddy footpaths, braving the thorns and the blades of grass that cut into their skin.

INTO THE TREES

They passed several small villages, but the natives just turned away. "Don't tell the soldiers," the bandits shouted at them in various languages—Yakan, Tausug, Tagalog.

The children cried constantly; the older ones comforted one another in whispers. The bandits did not talk. "Walk fast," was all they said, to the children. Those who stopped were kicked from behind.

Passing by a muddy creek, 14-year-old Chary Vergara scooped dirty water to quench her thirst. A bandit pushed her. "*Lakad na kung hindi mahuhuli tayo ng sundalo* (You walk or the soldiers will catch us)," the man said.

"That's better for me," she thought as she resumed walking.

The march was especially grueling for teacher Wenifer Silorio, eight months pregnant with her first baby.

When she slipped at the start of the trek, she saw the worried faces of Father Rhoel and Mr. Rubio. After walking a few kilometers, the bandits allowed her to sit down. When another group of armed men arrived with other hostages, Wenifer was ordered to stand up and walk.

"We're only thirty minutes away from our destination," a bandit assured them. But they had been walking for almost three hours already.

Wenifer was thirsty. "Can you give me water, please?" she asked the bandit nearest her.

"There's no water here," the man said, urging the teacher to walk faster instead.

They continued walking up and down the hills. They passed a murky river, and Wenifer was allowed to drink from it—floating insects, leaves, and all. When she was done, she found she was too tired to move. Her teacher-friend Anabelle tried to help her, but there was nothing much she could do. Wenifer's body had no more strength. Finally, she collapsed.

"Come on, Weng, let's go," she heard Anabelle urging her, but she could not move. She felt cold and her eyes were already failing her.

Then Wenifer heard the bandits dragging Anabelle away. Fear gripped her, but she could not do anything. A bandit dragged her until they arrived in a village where there was a motorcycle waiting. They put her on it. When they reached a river, however, the bandits decided to leave the motorcycle behind.

Then the men carried Wenifer—one for each leg and arm while another grabbed her hair. When they got tired, they dropped her on the ground and dragged her along again. She shouted and cried. The pain numbed her senses, and she lost consciousness again.

When they reached another river, the men plunged Wenifer into it, thinking that the cold water would revive her. In the river, she was aware of everything, but her body refused to cooperate. Back on dry land, but already wet and still half-conscious, she succumbed to an asthma attack. She could not breathe. Still she tried to walk, until she collapsed a third time.

The men looked for a blanket and laid Wenifer on it. Again they dragged her, the blanket too thin to protect her back against the rough ground—pebbles, stones, protruding roots. After some time, the blanket was completely torn, and the teacher's body was as tattered as the cloth.

"Ma'am, wake up. The soldiers are following us," a bandit said.

"Let us kill her now," another said. Tired and also exhausted, another man asked Wenifer to pray. "Ma'am, please pray. We are going to kill you."

"Make it quick, please," Wenifer murmured.

She prayed. "God, I entrust myself to you. They are going to kill me. If you want to get me now, please bring me to heaven."

Then she waited. Nothing.

"Don't kill her," Wenifer heard another bandit say. "Let us just leave her alone to the wild animals."

"But the surroundings are clean," another answered.

"It's all right, there are wild pigs here. They will finish her off," the first one said. Then they left her. She fell asleep praying.

She was awakened by the voices of other men, coming near her. They looked like they were teenagers, but like the others they were also armed. They picked her up and brought her to a house where they cooked food. There were women in the house, who helped her change her clothes. After she had rested, a woman approached her.

"Don't worry, Ma'am. They will carry you to camp," the woman said.

The young bandits placed her in a big basket and carried her until they reached the foot of Mount Punoh Mahadji at around eight o'clock in the evening. Wenifer was then brought to a house on a hill where an old woman, the mother of one bandit leader, lived. There were women in the house and they took care of the pregnant teacher. They fed her and massaged her body.

"*Manang,* my belly is aching," Wenifer cried. But the women did not understand. They spoke another language. She pointed to her stomach. An old woman approached her and massaged her belly. The whole night Wenifer did not sleep. The women kept watch on her; they did not sleep too.

THE BANDITS AND THEIR CAPTIVES reached Mount Punoh Mahadji late in the afternoon. The hostages knew they were already at their destination when they saw the sign: "Al Harakatul Islamia. Welcome to Camp Abdurazzak."

They continued climbing a few kilometers up the steep mountain, however, before they actually reached the camp.

Mr. Rubio helped Father Rhoel move forward. They were handcuffed together—the school principal's right wrist was linked to the priest's right wrist too. The handcuffs made it hard for them to walk side by side, but the position was also providential. Mr. Rubio was left-handed, so he was able to pull the priest up as they were climbing.

Before going up the camp, the kidnappers tightened the rope tied around Father Rhoel's waist and pulled him up. When the climb became too difficult, the bandits took the rope off and let the priest walk with the help of Mr. Rubio. The path was steep and slippery.

It was already dark when they entered the camp. Some of the hostages, especially the children, were already there. "Maybe they took another path," Mr. Rubio said later. It took him and Father Rhoel eight hours to reach the camp.

Abu Sabaya, the spokesman of the Abu Sayyaf who always wore dark sunglasses, approached Father Rhoel and Mr. Rubio. He took off the handcuffs. He did not say a word.

By the time everyone—kidnappers and captives alike—had settled down in the bandits' lair, the fog was thick. There were a lot of armed men, most of them obviously in their teens. They were all excited and agitated.

"Form a single line. We will kill you now," one man commanded.

The hostages followed.

"We're all tired and the military is nearby. Let's finish this," another said. "Form a line, fast!"

Then it started to rain. Instead of shooting the hostages, the bandits distributed biscuits and water to the nervous victims. They then led their captives to a hut that looked like a big box in the middle of a forest clearing. The door to the hut was on top. One had to climb up a wall and go down the other side to enter.

The windowless, wooden hut—measuring 12 feet by 38 feet, as Mr. Rubio determined later—would serve as the hostages' prison cell for almost two months. It looked like a monkey cage. It was divided into two: one side for the men, the other for the women. It was newly built, and had a toilet on each side.

Shivering in the cold night, the hostages lay down to rest in their wet clothes. They had no blankets; they felt the cold seep into their bones. Outside, wild animals howled. The rain poured like there was no tomorrow.

"Let us pray," Father Rhoel whispered.

IT WAS ALREADY DAWN when Wenifer fell asleep. When the cocks started to crow, she woke up. She felt ill. Her whole body was exhausted. Her asthma made it difficult to breathe. Her stomach was aching. "I will die now," she thought.

Late in the afternoon, a group of bandits arrived. "Ma'am, don't worry, the doctor is here," a young man said.

Red Cross volunteers arrived. They gave Wenifer some drug to ease her pain. A certain Dr. Lim, a Muslim, whispered to the teacher that the baby in her womb was still alive. Through her pain, Wenifer felt a stab of joy. Her "angel" was safe.

To prod the group into releasing her, the doctor made up a story.

"She has to be brought to a hospital. The baby in her womb is already dead. She will also die if she will not receive medication."

The armed men huddled in a corner. Wenifer waited nervously. Then the kidnappers came back, and said they had decided to let her go. The Red Cross volunteers rushed her to the capital town of Isabela. There, in the hospital, doctors told her that the child in her womb was in fact already dead.

"I felt so much hatred that I wanted revenge," Wenifer said later. "I wanted to recall the faces of all those who kidnapped me and wished them all dead, the same way they killed my baby. Why did they kill an angel?"

But Wenifer remembered what Father Rhoel always told the teachers at Claret Tumahubong. "Revenge is not good," he always used to say.

"So I entrusted to the Lord all the pain and suffering I went through and the feelings I had against the bandits."

THE HOSTAGES WERE AWAKENED by the sound of gunfire and rowdy shouting. Apparently, after their early morning prayers the Abu Sayyaf bandits fired their guns.

Later, someone called from the top of the hut, from the hole that served as door to the wooden prison. "You," the bandit pointed to Mr. Rubio, "come up here."

"Are you the priest?" the man asked the school principal when he was already on the roof of the box-like hut.

"No," Mr. Rubio said.

"But you are the oldest one here."

"He's the priest—Father Rhoel," Mr. Rubio pointed down to the priest silently sitting in one corner. "I am the school principal."

"Why are you calling him father? You are much, much older than him."

"Because he is a priest, a man of God," Mr. Rubio said.

The bandit was silent.

Later in the day, the bandits summoned Father Rhoel out of the hut.

"Abu Sabaya will interview you now," the bandit guarding the hut told Father Rhoel.

THIS IS HOW MR. RUBIO REMEMBERED Father Rhoel's first meeting with Abu Sabaya, as the priest recounted it to him.

"I WAS once a student of Claret College in Isabela," Abu Ahmad Salayuddin, a.k.a. Abu Sabaya, told Father Rhoel. "I even helped in the building of Monte Santo in Lamitan."

Monte Santo is a shrine on top of a hill. Catholics from Lamitan built a replica of the fourteen Stations of the Cross on the slopes of the mountain. On top stands a huge cross that is visible from nearby villages.

"How I regret ever helping to build it. Now I want the place razed to the ground. This place originally belonged to us Muslims. But we are being displaced. Even our religion is losing its hold on the island—all because of you Christians."

A Christian Yakan family in Lamitan adopted Abu Sabaya, then known as Aldam Tilao, when he was still young. He stayed with the family for twelve years. He sold copra on weekends and went to school the rest of the week, courtesy of the Christian family. The family described him as a good, humble young Moro. In his teens, Abu Sabaya left the family and studied engineering in Zamboanga. The family later learned that the child they treated as their own had gone to the Middle East to fight in some war. When he came back, the family observed that their adopted son was already a changed man. When they learned that Aldam Tilao had become the dreaded, outspoken Abu Sayyaf spokesman, they could not believe it. In the local tongue, Abu Sabaya's name means "thief of women."

"Your Catholic schools have corrupted our children. Look at the way our young women dress. You have influenced them with your distorted values! Basilan is ours! You Christians have no place in this island!"

Then he continued to lecture the priest about Islam, how it was introduced in the Philippines and how Christians discriminate against Muslims. He said the Abu Sayyaf wanted a separate Islamic state in Mindanao, the removal of crosses in Basilan, and the inclusion of Arabic teaching in the curriculum of all schools. "We also want all Muslim students to wear proper Muslim dress," he said.

When he was tired of talking, he asked the priest. "You, how did you become a Christian? Why are the Claretians in Basilan?"

"It is a long story," Father Rhoel said.

"We have all the time in the world," Abu Sabaya replied.

DURING THE FIRST FEW WEEKS of their captivity, the hostages were served meals regularly, consisting often of *tinapa*, *tabagak*, instant mami noodles, salt, chili, and water.

After a few weeks, food became scarce. Gone were the canned sardines, the tuna, the instant noodles.

Also, they could not sleep as much as they wanted to. They would wake up at five in the morning when the bandits gathered to pray and the camp stirred to life. The bandits would call the hostages using a megaphone.

The women and the children were regularly allowed outside the hut. The bandits let the children play and urged them to forget their cares. The women captives were asked to help prepare the meals. The male hostages were limited to the hut, although they too were allowed on occasion to stay on the roof for fresh air. Most of the time, however, they just played scrabble or play pretend basketball with an imaginary ball. It was during these moments when the hostages saw Father Rhoel unwinding, having fun.

Once, when they were so hungry, Mr. Rubio remembered he had been able to hide a yellow piece of Maxx menthol candy. The principal retrieved it, broke it, and then put it in the middle of the room. One by one, the hostages took a piece and drank a lot of water. Then they broke into laughter as tears rolled down their cheeks.

During days when they were not allowed to come out, the male hostages would follow the rays of the sun that entered the hut to keep warm. They also had light moments, especially during their first few days in the camp. They noticed personal mannerisms. Father Rhoel would reflexively comb his hair after coming out of the toilet; Mr. Rubio would instinctively tuck in his shirt. They used to make jokes about how they smelled. Later, however, they became used to it. "We smelled the same after a few days," Mr. Rubio said.

For their bath, Kipyong the man-child would fetch water for the male hostages. The public school teachers would promise him P5 per container, while Mr. Rubio and Father Rhoel promised P20 per because, as Mr. Rubio said, they "were from a private school." None of them, however, had any money. "We will pay you when we're free," they would tease Kipyong.

But Kipyong was happy with what he did for the teachers. He and the other children would play *palaka* and *syakay*, games children normally play in Basilan villages. The bandits also introduced the older children to the various guns they carried. They taught the children how to put bullets in the magazines and cartridges of M-16 and M-14 rifles. Sometimes the children were even allowed to shoot at the colorful birds hovering above the forest clearing.

The children were always free to move around and play. They even wandered up to the "high ground" where Janjalani, Sabaya, and the core of the Abu Sayyaf leadership stayed. The bandits, especially Janjalani, did not want to see the children crying. The children seemed to be enjoying themselves, too. They acted as if they were in a playground.

One day, public school teacher Lydda Ajon, who was abducted from the Sinangkapan Elementary School in Tuburan with husband Rosebert on the same day as the teachers from Claret, told the children to behave. "You think you're on vacation?" she scolded the children who had been running around the whole day.

A bandit heard her. Without any warning, the man slapped Lydda. "We don't want you ordering the children around," the man said.

"I was just telling them to behave," she said.

"Shut up! You don't have the right to give orders or to say what can and cannot be done here," the man shouted. "You are all prisoners here."

On another occasion Lydda was hit on the face by another bandit after she tried to ration out biscuits to the children. The man accused her of hiding the biscuits for herself and the older ones. "You are all the same here, not teachers, not students, but prisoners. Give the children everything. Let them have all they want," he said.

The children became friends with the bandits, most of whom were also very young. One bandit, for instance, was just a 12-year old boy, but he carried a "baby Armalite" rifle. Most of the Abu Sayyaf men didn't look menacing to the hostages. "In fact, they were ordinary-looking men except that they had firearms and they wore fatigues," Lydda later recalled. They would pray five times a day and were very religious. They never wore short pants.

Afterwards, Mr. Rubio also complained about the way the Abu Sayyaf spoiled the children. "Sometimes the children were really too much," the school principal said. "They ran around. When we called their attention, the Abu Sayyaf would get angry."

The bandits, it turned out, had been instructed to let the children feel at home, so they won't cry or scream and call the attention of the military. Some bandits, young as they were, also got tense every time the children cried.

In the evenings, some of the Abu Sayyaf would tell stories to the children. They would stay late laughing and exchanging jokes on the roof of the hut, to the consternation of the older captives who would suffer from the dust and pebbles falling on their faces below.

Abu Jar, a Chavacano Abu Sayyaf recruit, enjoyed telling the children stories he learned during his childhood in Zamboanga. He told his stories either in Bisaya or in Chavacano so that the children, mostly Bisaya-speaking, could understand.

"When you go back to your homes, make sure that you always look around or behind you because the monsters here in the forest will follow you," the children remember him saying more than once. The younger ones would instantly cry while the others would just smile or snicker in the corner.

Abu Jar also enjoyed talking about his childhood. He would advise the young boys not to court girls just yet because they were still too young. He would urge the children to take their studies seriously.

"But how could we study when we are here?" one Grade Six pupil asked.

"You will be released soon," Abu Jar assured them.

Another bandit taught the children Tausug songs. *Sari Bangkaw Tungtungon*, he would sing, and the children would repeat after him. Then they would teach the children Muslim prayers before going to sleep.

The children loved to tag along with the Chavacano Abu Jar, and the Visayans Abu Bilog and Abu Hapsin. Abu Jandal and Abu Mahamdi, a former public school teacher, taught the children how to play chess. They would tell the children that their kidnapping was not for money. "We just want our companions to be released from jail," they said. "You will be released soon," Abu Mahamdi said during the second week of the kidnapping.

Abu Sabaya also told the children that they would be released soon. "When you're home already, tell everybody to remove all the crosses in Basilan," Abu Sabaya told them. But the children were afraid of Abu Sabaya, Abu Tagalog, and the brother of Abu Jandal. "They were always angry at us," one of the children said later. All the while, Khaddafy Janjalani, the *amir*, would just sit silently in one corner.

The children loved to play "hide and seek." They said later they could have actually escaped if they wanted to, but were afraid to try, because the bandits said they had planted land mines in the area.

"They warned us not to go down the mountain because we would lose our feet," one survivor said.

The Abu Sayyaf always tried to convince the children to become Muslims. "Christians are dirty," the bandits would say. "Because you eat pork."

"We don't want to be Muslims," a seven-year-old answered one day. "Our tribe is Christian, and pork is good."

"Then we will kill you," one young bandit said in jest.

"Please, no!" another child pleaded. "We just don't know how to pray like Muslims."

"Convert to Islam! Abandon your faith and we will release you," the bandits replied.

When the hostages were alone in the hut in the evenings, the older ones would implore the children to hold fast to their faith.

"Even if they kill me, I won't give up being a Christian," Chary would always promise. Kipyong, however, usually kept silent. Later, he was seen praying with the bandits.

MOUNT PUNOH MAHADJI is beautiful. All around the place, as far as the eye can see, is virgin forest. One can see the whole of Basilan from the top.

The hostages loved looking at the distant sea, especially in the afternoon when the blue water looked so peaceful.

"God must really be here!" Father Rhoel said once, noting how the place was so serene and conducive for prayer. "Why not have one of our recollections here after we have been released?" he suggested to Mr. Rubio one day.

The verdant slopes of the mountain must have resonated with the contemplative in the priest. The idyllic surroundings, however, was a stark contrast to the dimly lit and poorly ventilated wooden prison of the hostages.

Camp Abdurazzak had three levels. On top of the mountain were the bunkers of Abu Sayyaf leaders. It was where Khaddafy Janjalani and Abu Sabaya stayed. The high-powered firearms and radio sets were all stored on the upper level, known to the hostages as the "high ground."

A few meters down was a clearing. In the center, surrounded by bunkers which were connected to each other by underground tunnels, was the hostages' hut. Most of the bandits stayed there. The ammunition bunker was also located there. A hut that served as kitchen was on one side of the clearing.

Farther down the mountain slope was a small Muslim village. A logging road, already covered with overgrowth, connected the village to the nearest town of Maluso. Government negotiators, Red Cross volunteers, and journalists who tried to contact the kidnappers later were allowed up to this village. It was known to locals as the "co-op," short for "cooperative," the organization of rubber plantation workers during the time of the multinational firms in the island.

IT WAS ON GOOD FRIDAY, April 21, more than a month after the abduction, and two days after public school teachers Nelson Enriquez and Dante Uban were "released," that the bandits finally called Mr. Rubio for an "interview."

First they let Mr. Rodolfo Irong out of the hut. Then, twenty minutes after Mr. Irong came back, Mr. Rubio was called. It was already about ten in the morning, but fog still covered the mountain camp.

About twenty meters from the hut where the hostages were held, in a bunker located on the "high ground," Khaddafy Janjalani, Abu Sabaya, and the other Abu Sayyaf leaders were waiting for the school principal.

"We will talk about your life," Abu Sabaya was the first one to speak. "We have demands, but the government is not responding. Can you give us one million pesos in exchange for your freedom?"

"Sir, I have children in college. I am the breadwinner of the family. I don't have money," Mr. Rubio said.

"We are talking about your life. If the military will attack Camp Abdurazzak, all male hostages will be executed one by one," Abu Sabaya said. The other bandits kept silent. Khaddafy was looking down at the ground, silently fingering a string of beads.

"So how much can you give?" Abu Sabaya asked.

"I have no money," Mr. Rubio said.

"But you have a lot of money. You are the principal of a private school," the bandit leader argued.

"I am only receiving P6,161 monthly," the school principal explained.

"One million pesos then," Abu Sabaya said. Khaddafy was still silent.

Rubio explained he could not afford to give the amount.

"How about P500,000?" prodded Abu Sabaya.

"Nothing," answered Mr. Rubio. "Maybe I can raise P50,000, but you need to release me so that I can borrow from my neighbors."

"No. We will just kill you and all the male hostages if the military will push through with their plan to take Punoh Mahadji by force," Abu Sabaya said.

"It's up to you. I can't do anything. But if you can, please spare our lives because we are innocent," the school principal said.

The bandits were silent.

"As a teacher in Claret, I have done a lot to help the Muslims. Many among your people became teachers. Others have even gone abroad and a lot more became professionals and are now working in government because of our mission."

"But you also Christianized a lot of Muslims," Abu Sabaya answered.

"I cannot remember a Muslim student who embraced Christianity because he studied in Claret," Mr. Rubio answered. "The mission of the Claretians is to educate the Muslims."

Mr. Rubio was born in Tumahubong. He started teaching at Claret Tumahubong in 1971, after graduating with a major in education at the Zamboanga A.E. Colleges, the same school where Abu Sabaya later studied engineering.

"Convert to Islam and you will be free," Abu Sabaya said. "Islam is good and it means well."

"There is no religion that does not mean well," Mr. Rubio answered. "But like taking a course in college, choosing one's religion is something that one has to think about seriously. You don't just choose any religion that you know nothing about. Maybe the time will come when I will eventually convert to Islam but this is not the right time."

Abu Sabaya looked at the direction of the silent Janjalani. The Abu Sayyaf leader was still looking down, still worrying the string of beads that looked like a rosary.

After he survived the ordeal, Mr. Rubio got hold of Janjalani's "rosary" and treasured it as a memento of his life in the hands of the Abu Sayyaf.

Janjalani reportedly grew fond of ten-year-old Jul, a young Grade Three pupil who was taken by Abu Sabaya from the elementary school in Tumahubong. When the military started bombarding the camp, and the bandits were already desperate to escape, Janjalani, whom friends and family call "Daf," gave the string of beads to Jul. When Rubio was rescued, he asked Jul for the beads.

"Why did Daf give it to you?" Mr. Rubio asked the boy.

"Daf said I looked like his son," Jul said. "He missed his young son a lot."

CHAPTER 4

IN THE TEDIUM OF THEIR ORDEAL, the past was a constant presence. There was no escaping it. Sometimes it came rushing like a flood after the monsoon rains. Even the bandits would fondly recall their families and friends and tell stories to the hostages.

In the evening, before they went to sleep, the children would talk about their parents or their brothers and sisters. They would laugh or cry, depending on the story. "*Madalas kami pumunta sa Zamboanga, halos tuwing Sabado't Linggo* (We used to go to Zamboanga every weekend)," one would recall. "My brother would tickle me before we went to sleep," another would say.

Father Rhoel had always been a good listener. He had a weak spot for the children, whom he fondly called the "little ones." In Tumahubong he played with the children who loitered outside the convent every afternoon. Much later, after his death, *Manang* Dolor remembered how the priest would go out of his way to play with them. Sometimes, Father Rhoel himself acted like a child. "I knew a lot of priests, but nobody had ever washed my hands except Father Rhoel, like he was my son," the blind woman said.

Atop Mount Punoh Mahadji, Father Rhoel would talk to the children and listen to their stories. He loved to learn from the "little ones" who seemed unmindful of the situation they were in. He promised the children he would bring them to Jollibee, the fast-food chain, when they were freed.

Listening to their laughter, he must have remembered his own childhood: the single-storey bungalow with its cemented patio; the vacant lot in front of the house where he used to plant flowers and fruit-bearing trees;

THE CLOUD ON THE MOUNTAIN- TOP

the white and pastel-colored orchids his mother tended during weekends; the small chicken house at the back; the mango tree he planted.

FATHER RHOEL was born on November 29, 1965 to engineer Dominador Gallardo and public school teacher Raquel Dayap. The future missionary was the second of five children. His sister Grace came before him, while his favorite brother, Dominador or "Junjun," came next, followed by Jesse and Edwin.

Because of her fondness for five-letter names, Raquel added an "h" to the name of her second son: thus, Rhoel. He was born in Olongapo City, on Luzon island, where his family lived at the time.

He was small compared to other children his age. When his grandmother tried to enroll him in kindergarten, the school refused to accept him. The teachers said he was too young and too small. He was six years old by then, but the eager grandmother had to wait for one more year to bring her grandson to school.

To the joy of the old woman, Rhoel spent a lot of time in his grandmother's house. She was fond of her *apo*, whom she said was very thoughtful.

"He was often with my mother when he was young because my husband and I were working," Raquel recalled after his death. "He used to sit by her side whenever she did the laundry. During *merienda*, he would bring his grandmother food to eat. He was around five years old then."

When Rhoel was ready for high school, the family decided to settle in Castillejos town, in Zambales province. "We waited for him to finish elementary school before we transferred," her mother said.

In Zambales, Rhoel went to the San Nicolas Academy. He spent his young adulthood in the quiet, laidback town of Castillejos until he decided to enter the minor seminary.

There, Rhoel struck his fellow seminarians as a silent, formal, and smart young man. His friends described him as the "serious type," although he did clown around. He had his own brand of "corny" humor. His high school classmates remembered him as the "witty but quiet fellow" who was ever ready to give advice. Because of his demeanor, he was dubbed the "father" of the class.

"He was very mature even as a child and was an obedient son. As the eldest son, he was very responsible," Raquel said. "You didn't need to ask help from him. In fact, even when he was already in college, he always volunteered to help me."

"I will be the one to cook, Ma," Rhoel would tell his mother. He was also very particular with the details, noticing even how, say, the curtains were hung.

As a student, Rhoel was average, but because he was very diligent in his studies, he won academic honors. He loved to read a lot and to play basketball. Unlike the other children, however, Rhoel went straight home after classes. He did not like going out in the evenings.

Rhoel was a protective brother. His mother remembered a time when a neighborhood toughie teased Junjun. When Rhoel heard the child laughing at a crying Junjun, the future missionary went after the kid.

When he was in college, Rhoel became even more self-reliant. Raquel remembered a time when three of her sons came down with chicken pox while studying at Saint Louis University in Baguio City. Jessie and Edwin went home to Zambales, but Rhoel decided to stay in the dormitory, enduring the pox alone.

He simply did not want to be a burden to anybody, even his family. "He did not want to be taken cared of. He did not want to be a burden to me because he had the pox. I felt very sad then. I cried because I wanted to take care of him. I felt useless. He did not go home until vacation time," Raquel said.

Rhoel was good at taking care of whatever money he had. His brothers and sister described him as "very thrifty." He looked after their finances when they were students in Baguio.

He was also very neat, tidy and organized with his things. But he had terrible penmanship. "It was readable but it needed much improvement," Raquel said. To improve her son's almost "unintelligible script," she told him to exercise his hands. She also asked Rhoel's teachers to give him writing exercises to improve his handwriting. "Good thing it improved through the years," Raquel said.

Like other teenagers, Rhoel had girlfriends, his mother said. But "he never told me anything," she said. "I would not be surprised if girls were after him, because he was good-looking, like his father."

After Rhoel's second year in high school, Father Cacho, an Agustinian priest, visited the Gallardo household and asked Dominador if he would allow his son to enter the St. Augustine Minor Seminary. Dominador said he would discuss the matter with his wife.

One night, after the family had turned the television set off and everyone was preparing for the night, fourteen-year-old Rhoel snuggled in between his parents. Had they already discussed Father Cacho's proposal, he wanted to know. Husband and wife just looked at each other, then asked their son: "Why, what do you really want?"

"I wish to enroll at the minor seminary for my third year in high school," Rhoel said.

"Do what you want. You have our support," Dominador told his son. What they did not know was that Rhoel had already finished packing his things and was all set to leave for the seminary the next morning.

After graduating from the minor seminary, however, Rhoel went home confused. He did not know what to do. He was not sure whether he wanted to push through with his seminary studies. Again, Dominador and Raquel let their son decide. "Think about it," Raquel said.

While on vacation, Rhoel busied himself tending to his plants in their backyard. In the end, he decided not to enroll at the major seminary. Instead, he took up Philosophy at Saint Louis in Baguio.

After graduation, however, he surprised his mother when he asked her to accompany him to the Claret Formation Center in Quezon City.

"I asked him where that was, he said he did not know either, but said a friend would accompany us," Raquel recalled. "I asked him if that was what he really wanted. He said Yes, so I gave him my blessing. I was surprised to see his things all packed. He had already decided."

Rhoel joined the Claretian missionaries as a seminarian on May 3, 1987—thirteen years, to the day, before his death. His parents brought him to see Father Angel Ochagavia, the vocation director. But two months later, when Dominador and Raquel visited him, Rhoel had changed his mind. He wanted to go home.

"It was raining hard that day. I noticed that he had lost weight and did not look happy. He told me he wanted to go home with us to Castillejos," Raquel said.

"I feel like I am losing my vocation," Rhoel told his mother.

He rode with his parents back to Castillejos that same day. In the evening, Rhoel told his mother he had apprehensions about pursuing his studies. He was not able to sleep until dawn.

"I always pray for you," she told him. In the morning, Raquel went to church and prayed for her son. "Lord, it is up to you. Whatever it is you want for my children, I will accept."

When Raquel came home, she was surprised to see Rhoel preparing his things to go back to Claret. "Thank you, Lord. If that's what he really wants, I will continue to support him," she prayed.

His decision brought much happiness to the family.

Missionary life for Rhoel started at Bunguiao in Zamboanga City, during his novitiate. His novice master, Father Emilio Pablo, observed that people in the villages appreciated Rhoel's apostolic spirit and initiative in conducting seminars.

"Little Claret," his fellow novices called him, because they thought his height and countenance made him look like Father-Founder Saint Anthony Mary Claret.

Rhoel took his first vows at the cathedral in Isabela, Basilan on May 1, 1989. He later served his "pastoral year" in Maluso and took his perpetual vows at Claret House in Quezon City on July 16, 1993.

In his application for his perpetual profession, Rhoel wrote: "My pastoral immersion in Basilan made me experience concretely our witnessing and evangelizing life and mission as well as our community's presence in the dialogue of life and faith with our Muslim brothers and sisters."

"These experiences have become a real challenge to me to be a committed missionary and an active witness to God's liberating love for humanity, conscious that our life and mission demand a total giving of ourselves for the greater glory of God and the salvation of humankind."

He was ordained deacon at the Santo Niño Parish church in Surabay, Zamboanga del Sur, a Claretian mission. Rhoel was ordained priest at the Immaculate Heart of Mary Parish in Quezon City on December 8, 1994. After his ordination, Father Rhoel was sent back to Surabay, once a village of Ipil town, for his first mission. While he was there, the Abu Sayyaf attacked Ipil, razing it to the ground and killing at least 53 people.

When he had the time, the young priest would go home to Castillejos. "Every time he comes home for a vacation, he would go around town first and visit friends before coming to the house. He was very well-loved here," his mother said.

During one such vacation, neighbors asked the young priest to stay in Zambales and serve as a diocesan priest. But he was happy being a missionary, he said. Back in Surabay, he wrote his family: "I am happier here, with the poor people."

In 1999, after bandits killed a group of catechists in Tumahubong, Basilan on Valentine's Day, Father Rhoel volunteered to be parish priest. When his mother learned of it, she wrote her son, "Isn't it dangerous there?"

A few weeks after his arrival in Tumahubong, the new priest started receiving threats from the Abu Sayyaf. The bandits demanded a donation of P10,000 a month from the Claretian mission. Despite the danger, Father Rhoel did not complain. He did not mind the work. He cooked his own food and did his laundry.

Father Rhoel's last visit to his family, in January 2000, was a memorable one for his mother. "I met him at the gate and he hugged me very tightly like he had never done before. Grace noticed that and wondered," Raquel said.

He was happy to see his nephews and nieces again and even volunteered to take care of them. "One afternoon, I wondered why it was very noisy in their room. Then I saw him playing with the kids. He was having a great time. He had skipped his siesta, which he rarely did in the past, unless he had something very important to do," Raquel said.

Every time Rhoel came home for vacation he would stay in the living room, spread a mat on the white marble floor, and lie down listening to his favorite songs on the stereo. When he was not resting, he would either cook, oftentimes inventing recipes, or go around the garden to check on his mango tree or pull out the weeds.

At times, he would stay in the porch at the back of the house, often scribbling notes in his diary or simply enjoying the afternoon breeze in his favorite old rattan rocking chair.

THE COOL BREEZE brought the priest back to his senses. It was one of those rare evenings during their ordeal when the guards were not too strict and the male hostages were allowed to stroll outside the hut.

Sitting on the rough planks of wood that served as the roof of their makeshift prison, Father Rhoel exclaimed, "God must really be here in these mountains."

"Shhhh, they might hear you," Mr. Rubio said, pointing to the armed men around them.

"Look at the sunset, look at those evening stars, look at the trees, the mountain. This must be paradise," the priest answered. "We can have one of our recollections here after our release."

"I hope so," Mr. Rubio answered. "I hope it will be soon, Father."

Waving his hands as if touching the landscape, the priest said, "Look over there, Mr. Rubio. See the ocean? There is Maluso. I spent my pastoral year there."

The school principal kept silent.

"Can you hear that?" Father Rhoel said, excitedly. "Furaydah is singing again."

Furaydah was a young Bajau mother Father Rhoel had met. She sang melancholy songs to lull her six-month-old daughter to sleep.

Father Rhoel recounted how he watched 14-year-old Hanang, she with the expressive eyes and long black hair, weeping while listening to Furaydah's songs. Her handsome Misdal, whom she had married only five months before, was gone, lured by the *saitan*, the evil spirit, to leave his young wife and join the Abu Sayyaf. Hanang had their baby aborted.

"It would be a shame for her to have a child without a father," Father

Rhoel told Mr. Rubio. "The child would have died, because she would not have been able to feed it. But even in death, she has a problem. Her tribe has no more burial place."

"You know their story, Father?" Mr. Rubio asked. "You've been on the island for only a year."

"Theirs is a sad story," the priest said, "a very, very sad story."

INSPIRATION MADE HIM a missionary. The example of priests who had gone before him sustained him in his mission.

On June 8, 1994, the Abu Sayyaf abducted diocesan priest Cirilo "Loi" Nacorda. Father Rhoel followed Loi's story like it was his own. Later, he heard Father Loi himself recount his experience before other priests during a retreat in Basilan.

Father Loi and his driver were on their way to Matarling from Isabela; it was around 7:30 a.m. and they were only a few kilometers away from his parish. His driver overtook two jeeploads of teachers on their way to school. The teachers waved at the priest as his jeep rushed by.

When they reached Kilometer 12, Father Loi saw armed men in the middle of the street. A log was blocking the road. He told his driver to stop, and the armed men approached the vehicle. "This is just a bad dream," the priest thought. He knew Father Bernardo Blanco, the Spanish Claretian missionary, was kidnapped on the same stretch of highway only the year before.

The men were all in military uniform, and some were wearing masks. A bandit, who introduced himself as *Kumander* Kalaw, approached the passenger side of the jeep. The others started breaking the windshield with the butt of their rifles. "This is for real," Father Loi realized.

"I am just thirty-seven years old, newly ordained, barely two years into the ministry. God, is this my end?" The thoughts raced through his head. The bandits forced him to get down from the jeep and struck him in the stomach and on the side with the butt of an M-14 rifle. They pointed their guns to his head and told him to kneel on the ground. They tied his hands behind his back and took his wallet.

When the bandits saw his identification card, they were ecstatic. "So, you're a priest," the commander said.

"Yes, I am a priest," he answered.

"Then we hit the jackpot," *Kumander* Kalaw said. "We planned to kidnap teachers but now we have a priest."

Father Loi could not speak. He turned and saw his driver; he was bound too. They were brought about fifty meters into the forested roadside. He thought the bandits would kill them at any moment. Pointing their rifles at them, the bandits ordered him and his driver to kneel.

"This is our end. Let us pray and hope that even if we die we will end up in purgatory and we will have a chance to go to heaven," he told his driver.

After two or three minutes, another group of armed men arrived, herding the teachers and students who were on board the two passenger jeeps Father Loi had overtaken at Kilometer 8. In all, there were some seventy hostages. The group walked for about two kilometers and then stopped. The bandits asked the hostages who among them were Muslims. They were released. Among the Christians left behind, the bandits released only the children and the old ones.

The bandits started asking the remaining hostages who among them could afford to pay ransom. Those who said they could not pay because they were poor, including the priest's driver, were separated from the group. Father Loi was not asked; the bandits later told him they were confident the government would pay for a kidnapped priest. They also retained the teachers, those who promised to pay ransom.

Including the driver, there were sixteen poor hostages gathered on one side. The bandits took the strings of the crucifixes they found in the priest's jeep to tie them up. They trampled on the crucifixes and stepped on Father Loi's sick call kit, which contained the oil for the sick and the chrism. This maddened the priest, but he could not move.

After they tied the sixteen hostages individually with the nylon necklaces, they took the rope of a carabao that was pastured nearby and used it to tie them together. "We will tie them together because we will release them. The rope will slow them down and they cannot run and tell the authorities where we are going," a bandit explained.

They then ordered everyone else to start walking toward the forest, into the mountain. After about thirty minutes, the hostages reached a small hut in the middle of the forest, where they were told to rest. It was then that they heard the shots.

Some of the teachers started crying, thinking it was a rescue operation and they would be caught in the crossfire. One of the bandits said it was indeed a rescue operation and soldiers were shooting it out with the bandits nearby. But after two to three minutes, the firing stopped.

When they reached camp later, Father Loi heard the bandits talking to each other.

"The other one's skull was broken," one said.

"I cut off the penis of the other," another boasted.

"Shut up, both of you," another man said as he showed off a bunch of peso bills. "You didn't see the old man? He had a lot of money in his wallet."

"This jacket belonged to the policeman," another proudly said.

"I got a ring," one added.

"I have a new watch," another one said.

Father Loi tried to hold back his tears.

The other hostages who were brought to the bandits' camp stayed in the mountains for only five days. They suffered a lot but survived the ordeal. Father Loi, however, spent 61 days in the mountains.

Unlike Father Rhoel and the hostages from Tumahubong, Father Loi was moved from camp to camp as the Abu Sayyaf tried various hiding places. The priest tried to talk to his captors. But most of the time, he just kept quiet, observing the group.

"I pretended to sleep and listen to their conversations. I learned a lot from them, their plans, their connections, their victims," the priest would say later. But he was always tied. Sometimes even his feet were tied. There were times he was chained to a house post.

A certain Ustadz Ben once engaged him in a debate. "Islam is peace and Islam is for justice," Ustadz Ben said.

"If Islam is really for peace and for justice, why are you killing innocent people? Is this for peace? Are you doing justice to us?" the priest angrily answered.

The kidnappers thought the priest did not understand Tausug and Yakan. He pretended he was only beginning to learn the languages from his captors and the bandits believed him.

"Christians are really intelligent, they learn fast," one said in Tausug. The bandits did not know that Nacorda was born and grew up in Basilan.

Although the bandits continued to be hostile to him, Father Loi was able to establish a relationship with them. They learned to respect his humility and submissiveness. He always offered to help cook their food. He boiled cassava and helped gather firewood or fetch water even if his feet were chained and his hands loosely tied. He cleaned their camp.

The bandits admired the priest. They said their leaders—the *ustadz* and *imam*—did not do those chores. One bandit commented that priests were different because they knew how to cook, fetch water, and even gather firewood.

There were times when, before the bandits left to ambush soldiers or after they arrived from a military encounter, Father Loi boiled water so that they could have something hot to drink. He would prepare coffee or tea for them, even though the dirty water from the river looked like chocolate, especially during rainy days.

Father Loi learned to survive by drinking the same dirty water and eating cassava and papaya. There were times they had *camote* (sweet potatoes) or chicken from abandoned villages.

Most of the time, especially when they were already on the run, they would sleep on the ground. There were many military encounters and ambushes; Father Loi could not imagine how he survived them all. The daily conditions alone were torture. There were times he was told to prepare himself because he was about to be killed. Other times the bandits would make fun of him and use him as target when they practiced throwing knives.

The priest tried to understand them. They were really fundamentalists, he thought. They were serious about their faith and always prayed and talked about defending Islam. Later, however, he realized they were out only to make money. They only used Islam as a front. It was easy for them to recruit followers because they offered huge sums to entice people to join them.

At some point, it was reported in the media that Father Loi had already joined the bandits, and that in fact he was allowed to carry a gun. It happened after journalists visited the bandits a month after his kidnapping. When they asked him if it was true that many bandits had been killed in military operations, Father Loi said the reports were not true.

He told the journalists that despite the bombings and the ambuscades, only two bandits had been wounded and nobody had been killed. The wounded were brought to Jolo. The priest did not know that he was being interviewed on camera and that what he was saying was being recorded. He thought the journalists were only taking his picture.

He also didn't know then that he was about to be released. Barahama Sali, the Abu Sayyaf leader who abducted him, later said the priest was scheduled that day to be released, but negotiations did not push through because the government did not meet the bandits' demand of P4 million. Barahama said government negotiators were only able to raise P1 million.

Later, the bandits told him that his statement had angered the military. They said the soldiers were now hunting him down too.

At first Father Loi did not believe them, but a military encounter three days later convinced him. He saw that the soldiers did not care anymore if the hostage was hit. It was no longer a rescue operation but a "search and destroy" operation.

He asked the Abu Sayyaf for a gun. He said that because the government wanted him dead, he ought to help the bandits survive.

He asked Barahama, who was already friendly with him, and he was given an Armalite. He found out, however, that the gun had no firing pin. They did not know that he knew how to use guns.

"*Brod*, why is it that your gun has a firing pin and mine has none?" he asked.

They laughed and gave him a firing pin. They asked him not to put a bullet in the chamber, however. Later, they trusted him enough to make him carry an M-203 rifle. They said they wanted him to be safe and avoid being identified by the military during encounters.

Father Loi did carry a rifle, but it was slung on his shoulder. He really did not want to shoot any soldier.

Carrying the rifle that way, he would walk with Barahama in front of him. Hadji, another bandit who became a friend, was behind him, and Mauran walked beside him.

They were walking in that formation when soldiers fired at them.

A blast shook the earth, and Father Loi was thrown about three meters off the ground. Many bandits were hit, including Barahama. Father Loi immediately crawled to retrieve his rifle.

(He later learned from the soldiers who ambushed them that he had really been their target. They had thought he was the leader of the group because he was wearing a *kopya*, a Muslim pilgrim's cap. The soldiers admitted, however, that they could not understand why they could not hit him.)

The priest was sure he was hit, but he was not even wounded. There wasn't even a scratch.

He lay on his stomach as bullets rained on them. Then something inexplicable happened. He saw the bullets passing in front of his face as if in slow motion, just like in the movies. "Maybe I am dead or I am having some kind of hallucination," he thought. He touched his body, his face.

He got his rifle and crawled toward Barahama. The commander was still alive and was shooting back at the soldiers. After a few minutes, however, the dreaded Barahama Sali collapsed. Before he closed his eyes to die, he told the priest: "You go now, Father. You escape."

He started to make a run for it but realized he could not move. He could not even crawl because of the volume of fire. "This is the end," he thought. He remembered he had a spare T-shirt in the knapsack on his back. He took the bag and covered his head with it, knowing full well that it could not protect him from the bullets. He also took the plastic water container he was carrying, though he realized it could not even protect him from a bolo.

It was a moment of surrender to the Lord. "If I will die here I will accept it, but this I ask, please give me a place in your kingdom," Father Loi prayed. He recited the act of contrition and started confessing his sins. "Lord, I'm sorry for all my sins. Please forgive me, Lord. I hope you will still accept me."

He bowed his head and kissed the ground. He waited for a bullet to hit him. But after about three minutes, he realized that the shooting had died down. He touched his head and his body to make sure he was still alive. "Why wasn't I hit?" he wondered.

Bullet shells littered the ground, but he did not even have so much as a scratch. He had counted at least 14 or 15 bullets fall to the ground in front of his face. He wondered why none struck him.

Then he remembered that while the shooting was going on, he saw some kind of smoke. He thought it was merely smoke from the firearms, but it was a thin cloud surrounding him.

(Months later, when he recounted his experience with some monks, they told him that that was the mantle of the Blessed Virgin Mary.)

It was not the first time he enjoyed that protection. During his first month in captivity, he was caught in the middle of an intense firefight between the military and the Abu Sayyaf. Helicopter gunships unloaded on the camp for almost three hours. Father Loi, chained to the post of a hut, prayed hard. "I hope you will help me, I hope I will be rescued."

"Lord, please help the soldiers, I hope all the Abu Sayyaf here will die."

Then he turned and saw the bandits praying too. "*Allahu Akbar*," they shouted. "Do not abandon us. Do not let the soldiers win this war."

Moved by pride, Father Loi wanted to tell the Abu Sayyaf: "Your God will not protect you, stupid fools. You are animals! I believe that God will listen to me and not to your prayers."

It was around three in the afternoon, and it was unbearably hot. Suddenly, a dark cloud covered the place. It was eerie. The fog in the mornings was a thin mist; the cloud that afternoon was as thick as a mantle.

Father Loi could hardly believe it. "Lord, thank you for helping the soldiers. Now the Abu Sayyaf will not see them."

But when the shooting stopped, Father Loi was stunned by what he saw. About 30 soldiers were dead. He saw them with his own eyes, including the officer whose nametag read "Lt. Juljuli." Only two bandits were wounded, however.

The priest felt as if lightning had hit him. He cursed the Lord. "What kind of God are you? Maybe you are a God of the Abu Sayyaf. You are a God of crazy people, of kidnappers and rapists. I don't want you anymore! I don't believe in you anymore! You are no longer the God of my life!" He was crying.

If he had not been tied to the post, he would have grabbed a gun and shot all the bandits in sight. He wanted to avenge the death of the soldiers; at the same time, he was consumed by a hatred of God.

"What kind of God are you? You don't even listen to your servant. You abandoned me! You are not the Christian God I know!" he shouted at the heavens.

He did not pray for weeks.

Finally, in the depths of despair, he started conversing with the Blessed Virgin Mary. Later, using his fingers, he prayed the rosary. He told the Virgin Mary about his hatred for her son. "I hate Jesus Christ. I don't want your son anymore. He is not God."

He talked to her, and he talked to St. Joseph, and he talked to the other saints. Once, he even talked to the Holy Spirit. He caught himself, and started laughing. "Jesus is of course part of the Holy Spirit. But in the mountain, my theology was destroyed," he would say later.

After he survived his ordeal, he asked the Lord for pardon. "I'm sorry for losing my faith and trust in you. I sinned against you, I'm sorry. I hope you will forgive me and I hope you can still accept me in your kingdom." He bowed his head and again kissed the ground.

ON MOUNT PUNOH MAHADJI, darkness swallowed the forest. The silence of the night seemed to reach the heavens. The children were silent, and the women too. Some of the men were already snoring, and the guards were sitting in their bunkers.

"Time to rest, Father," Abu Mahamdi, a former teacher who joined the bandits, told Father Rhoel. "It's getting cold already. The cold wind is bad for the head. It makes one remember the past. It's not good to be lonely here, especially now that we have nothing much to eat."

"Yes, I'm going to sleep now," Father Rhoel said.

Inside the hut, he lay down beside the other male hostages.

"Are you going to sleep now, Father?" Mr. Rubio asked.

"Not yet," he said. "Let us pray." They prayed the rosary in whispers. The other hostages who were still awake joined them.

Before he closed his eyes to sleep, Mr. Rubio heard Father Rhoel still praying. "I'm sorry, Lord, for everything that I have done," he heard him say.

THE SLOW BOAT

ALEJANDRO INFANTE is an 87-year-old doctor who emigrated to Basilan with the nurse of his dreams just two months before the start of the war in the Pacific.

"We came on a slow boat. It was in the morning. It was a bright, sunny day. I could see a round ball of mass of land. Green, it was all green. And then as we approached, I thought the whole island was all forest because what were glaring at us were trees. Trees that I had never seen in my life. I saw trees in my hometown in Bulacan—sampaloc tree, mango tree, duhat tree, bamboo tree, papaya tree, banana tree, rice tree, whatever. But here, it was different. Oh boy, I was surprised, the trees were very big. I was surprised. And when we had a chance to go to town in the evening days later, I saw herds of wild things crossing the streets, suddenly appearing in front of us—wild deer, monkeys, and birds, plenty of birds. It's a beautiful place."

Alejandro and his pregnant wife Susan landed in Basilan on October 2, 1941. "It was all an interrelationship of events," Alejandro would say later.

"The town of Isabela—you could not call it a town—looked like a barrio. There were not so many people and the roads were muddy; the houses were nothing. No concrete, nothing. It was all forest, solid forest, despite the lumbering of the Americans and the logging to give way for the plantation of rubber trees. The island was all forest."

Alejandro is a Tagalog from Bulacan who ventured to Mindanao after finishing his medical studies at the University of Santo Tomas in Manila. He wanted to work in the fabled southern islands of the Philippines, where people lived on colorful *vinta* and made love in their canoes.

But Alejandro ended up circumcising twelve-year-olds as a medical intern at the Zamboanga General Hospital; it was not what he had in mind. It was in that hospital, however, where he met Susan; they married four months and eight days later, on February 10, 1941, her birthday. Alejandro was 26; Susan, 23. Together, their monthly salary amounted to P45.

But in Basilan, an island just across the sea from Zamboanga, opportunities fell like the monsoon rains—or so his new friends said. He thought of going there to catch some for himself.

With the logic he learned from the Dominicans at the university, the father-to-be convinced his wife to quit her job as a nurse and come with him to the jungles of Basilan. After much haggling and cajoling, Susan gave in.

"There were Zamboangueños, some Visayans, a few Tagalogs. The native Yakans were very friendly people. They wore a colored piece of cloth around their waist where they hang their bolos and keep their *buyo* and *mama*. They went to work in tight pants, which were very colorful. They were so friendly. That was their kind. Some of them [I met] are still alive. But they're very, very old. The Yakans are Muslims, but there are other Muslims, the Tausugs. They came from Jolo."

When Japan bombarded Zamboanga on January 1, 1942, Alejandro and Susan watched the planes strafe and bomb the city from their mountain hiding place in Basilan.

The couple remembered their friends in Zamboanga, but they could not do anything. Villagers from all over Basilan repaired to the mountains. Panic was widespread.

Alejandro and Susan went deeper into the forest. The natives welcomed them in Panunsulan, deep in Basilan.

"We never had any problems with the natives. Most of them were Muslims. We were so lucky. We would mingle with them. They had access to the sea, so they provided us dried fish. They stayed close to the sea. Some were Tausugs, some were from other ethnic groups. The Yakans were [really] pagans. They stayed more in the farms while the Tausugs stayed by the sea. The natives were the original settlers of Basilan before the conquerors came."

Susan delivered her child in the mountains during the war. When she could not offer her baby milk because of the stress she was under, Alejandro and his Muslim friends looked for goats to feed the newborn baby. When the goats refused to give milk, a Muslim neighbor offered him a herd of cattle.

After the war, Alejandro and Susan worked for an American lumber company and were able to save enough money. Several years after that, in 1951, the vision that brought Alejandro to Basilan became real. The couple set up the Infante Hospital in Isabela to serve their Muslim friends in the mountains.

It was in their small hospital where the couple witnessed the brutality of war.

"Muslims wanted to claim Basilan as their own. They wanted the Christians to leave Basilan. It is a sentiment that was handed down from generation to generation since the beginning of time. It's easy to understand. There were no Christians before in Basilan. Why is it that there are Christians here now? Why is it that Christians own big pieces of land and hold high positions in government? This land is ours, the Muslims say. Even educated Muslims believe in that. They've gotten to hate the Christians. Christians are also arming themselves. The people are divided. Government should prevail and take control. But authorities are very slow."

Alejandro remembered his friend, Bishop Querexeta. "Christians called him a Yakan because he was so concerned about the welfare of the natives." Querexeta even chose to become a Filipino citizen to be with the people of Basilan and serve the poor, especially the Muslims. The bishop had many projects and never tried to convert a single Muslim. The bandits praised him for it.

When he left in July 1998 for a vacation in Spain, the bishop told Alejandro, "Doctor, I'll come back soon. I hope I can bring some money for our projects. I will not stay long there. As soon as possible I will come back."

But the bishop did not come back. He died in Spain a few months after he left Basilan—a century after the Spanish colonial government turned over the island to the Americans.

"Nothing changes, nothing ever will," Alejandro whispered, as he slowly closed his eyes and rested his head on Susan's shoulders.

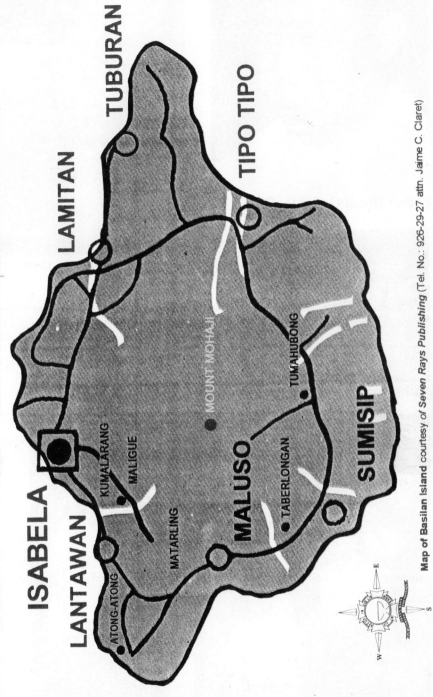

BASILAN ISLAND

(REGION IX: WESTERN MINDANAO)

ISABELA

LANTAWAN

LAMITAN

TUBURAN

TIPO TIPO

• ATONG-ATONG

KUMALARANG

• MALIGUE

MATARLING

MOUNT MOHAJI

TUMAHUBONG

• TABERLONGAN

MALUSO

SUMISIP

Map of Basilan Island courtesy of Seven Rays Publishing (Tel. No.: 926-29-27 attn.: Jaime C. Claret)

Father Rhoel Gallardo, CMF

Manong Emiliano's Jeep

Father Loi *(right)* with an Abu Sayyaf guard

Chary

Marissa

Wenifer

Mr. Rubio

Anabelle

Father Rhoel and Claret School Teachers: *(L-R)* Marissa, Marilou, Joy, Angie, Analyn, Gloria, Anabelle, Wenifer

Editha

Abu Sabaya and Khaddafy Janjalani

Abu Sayyaf Bandits whoop it up *(top)* and face the press *(left)* Philippine Army soldiers patrol Basilan *(below)*

Claret School
Graduates,
Class of 2001

Claret School of Tumahubong

Father Rhoel's office
at Claret School

Bishop De la Cruz

MOUNT PUNOH MAHADJI's beauty is deceiving, its shadow treacherous. Its sound is the wailing of its victims, its breeze the breath of the dying.

In a savage world like Mount Punoh Mahadji, only those who find the strength survive.

Marissa Rante's test of will began on Monday, April 10, the 21st day of her ordeal at the hands of the Abu Sayyaf. Early that morning, the bandits took her and separated her from the other hostages. They did not tell her where they were bringing her.

"*Siguro ililipat nila ako para makapahinga dahil may sakit ako* (I am sick, maybe they will bring me somewhere where I can rest)," she thought as a blindfold was put on her face. She was not afraid. She was sick and exhausted, and was willing to die if rest lay in death.

She was not running a fever. She was just plain tired. She had not been eating, because she was not hungry. She looked pale.

"Where are you taking me?" she asked.

"You will be given medical attention," a bandit answered.

"Let me go with her," Anabelle said.

"Don't," Marissa intervened. "Take care of your sister Romela."

Marissa started to walk, guided by an Abu Sayyaf bandit. They did not hold her hand because it was taboo for a Muslim man to hold an unmarried woman's hand, so they let her hold on to a piece of cloth which they used to pull her up.

IN THE
HEART
OF
DARKNESS

They were walking up, toward the "high ground." "They're bringing me to their leaders," she thought. Instead, she was put inside a hut near the bunkers of the Abu Sayyaf leaders, where Khaddafy Janjalani, Abu Sabaya, and the rest of the commanders lived.

Then it hit her. She was the only woman on the "high ground." She was alone, lonely, and scared. She thought of committing suicide; instead she prayed.

Then something "bad" happened to her, once, then twice, then more times, she would later say. "I will never forget that time."

THE MORNING MARISSA WAS TAKEN by the bandits, Lydda Ajon was distributing breakfast to the children. She was counting the biscuits to give to the children when she heard the bandits arguing with Marissa and Anabelle. She immediately went to the corner of the hut.

"Rosebert, Rosebert," she called her husband, whispering.

"What?" her husband answered on the other side.

"They're taking Marissa away, alone," she said.

"Where?"

"I don't know. Maybe down to the cooperative. They said they're bringing her somewhere to rest," she said.

Rosebert turned to tell the other male hostages in the room, but they had already heard Lydda. The men were angry. "Where are they taking her?" they asked.

Father Rhoel shouted at the guards. "Where did you bring Marissa? Why did you take her alone?"

Abu Jandal, the leader of the guards that day, heard the priest. The college-student-turned-Abu Sayyaf-bandit peered down from the top of the hut.

Mr. Rubio, the principal, saw the bandit first. "Tell Father Rhoel to calm down," Mr. Rubio whispered to Nelson Enriquez. Nobody wanted to approach the already angry priest. Maybe Nelson, the oldest among the hostages, could do it. He knew how to sweet-talk even the bandits; he could communicate in several languages.

Nelson approached the priest and whispered to him. The priest calmed down, but by then it was too late. Abu Jandal was angry now, and staring at them straight.

"Don't think ill of us, Father. We will not harm Marissa," Jandal said from the top.

The priest grumbled and turned away.

"Why are you like that, Father? Trust us. We will treat Marissa well. We know that she is sick. We will give Ma'am Marie medication," Jandal said.

MARISSA'S PARENTS migrated to Basilan from Bohol in the 1960s. Their daughter was born in Tumahubong.

She grew up in the village with eight other siblings. Poverty—eating only once or twice a day—was not new to her. As a kid, she had gone with the others into the forest to "evacuate" when Moro rebels invaded their village.

The young teacher was close to the church. Her family actually lived a spitting distance from the door of the convent. "If you stay in a barrio and you want to have something to do, you help in the church," she would say. During the time of the kidnapping, she was preparing for the patron saint's feast day.

The bandits took her on March 20 because she looked too innocent to devise an escape plan. She was inside her classroom in Claret School when she heard a shot. She looked out the window and saw men in black. Her students cried out. "Ma'am, hide. The bandits are here."

Muslim students hid her by lying on top of her and covering her with their skirts. When a bandit entered, the students said their teacher was already gone. But when the armed men told the Muslim students they could go home, the children scampered downstairs, and the bandits found poor Marissa on the floor.

She was thankful that other teachers had been abducted, too; she was not alone. The women gave her a *turong*, a veil, because the bandits did not like her school uniform. It showed some white skin, they said.

In the evenings, she slept beside fellow Claretian teacher Anabelle; the two used their *turong* to tie their hands together. That way, if one of them were taken out during the night, the other would wake up and help.

After a few days in captivity, Marissa was allowed out of the hut. She, Anabelle, and Lydda would sometimes cook for the rest of the hostages. She also found that some of the bandits were nice to her. But she later said she did not know if they had been sincere. They called her Ma'am, and asked her why she was a Christian.

"You are wrong to believe in Jesus Christ," a bandit said. "Jesus is just human," another joined in.

But Marissa did not take the bait. She knew they wanted to weaken her faith. "Why did you take us?" she replied instead. "We are not rich."

"Claret School is rich," the bandits said. They also said the teachers were agents "out to destroy Muslim values."

"We do not teach anything against Muslims," Marissa said.

ON APRIL 11, at around 10:30 a.m., the bandits went to teach the priest a lesson for making a scene the previous day. The male hostages were playing scrabble inside the hut.

"Tie the priest down," they shouted from above as they threw a piece of rope down. "Push him up," the bandits ordered when they saw the priest was already bound.

Sinangkapan teacher Ruben Democrito pushed Father Rhoel up while a bandit pulled from above. When the priest staggered out onto the roof, a kick in the stomach greeted him even before he could smell the soothing breeze.

In the distance, the children were playing; some were watching him. He tried to stand up, but when he looked up the rays of the sun that penetrated the thick branches of the centuries-old trees blinded him.

He stumbled. A bandit struck him on the back with a rifle's butt. He tried to stand up, but someone kicked him in the face. His eyes swelled, and there was blood in his mouth. He was helped up, but again punches rained on his face and belly.

"What did I do?" the priest asked.

"Nothing," the bandits said, laughing.

"You better pray to your God now!" barked one of the bandits. "Let us see if your crosses will save you."

"The cross is a sham, you only created your God out of the cross. It's either you convert to Islam or we'll behead you," another said.

Father Rhoel looked miserable. Tears rolled down his cheeks. His already swollen lips were trembling.

"Non-believers of Islam are our enemies!" the bandits shouted as they continued to kick the hapless man. They spit, hit, and cursed him, like he was a stray dog.

"Kidnapping and killing you won't risk our souls. When we die we will go to heaven," the bandits taunted him.

"I could kill you right now," a bandit said.

"You are not a priest here. You are our prisoner. We are the law here," the bandit named Sayyaf shouted at the fallen priest.

"Are you ready to die?" Sayyaf added as he prodded the priest's stomach, and then his head, with his M-14.

"Now try to pray to your God to see if he will listen to you," the bandit named Abdulazziz said.

MARISSA'S RECOURSE was prayer. She could hear the bandits laughing. But she was afraid to look outside. She was afraid, constantly afraid, so she just prayed.

"What if one of the bandits would find me attractive?" she had asked her-self before. "Who knows what they would do to me?"

Earlier, one of the bandits introduced himself as a former classmate in col-lege. He apologized to Marissa, saying he was just doing his job. Later, he asked Marissa's hand in marriage. She refused.

Marissa was transferred again. She thought it was for an interrogation, but she was brought to a place where there was nobody but herself. Then Abu Sabaya entered the room. Marissa was scared. She saw tablets on a table in a corner. She thought of taking it all and ending her life. But she could not do it. She prayed.

Every time someone came near her, she would tremble in fear. They would give her food, they would allow her to walk, but they seemed to have plans for her. (In the newspapers, it was already being reported that Marissa had gotten married to Abu Sabaya and her parents had already received thou-sands of pesos in dowry.)

During one of her walks around the camp, Marissa saw that one of their *barangay* captains (village heads) in Tumahubong had an Abu Sayyaf com-mander for a brother. She also saw some of her Muslim neighbors. They were all Abu Sayyaf members. Some of her students were Abu Sayyaf mem-bers, too. They carried big guns like big men. It was a nightmare, she thought.

A few days later, her things—toothbrush, blanket, and clothes—were brought to her. The bandits said she would have to stay in the mountain for good. Marissa cried. "I want to be with the others," she insisted. The bandits refused. Then Abu Sabaya arrived. He visited her at least five times, sometimes with Khaddafy Janjalani, the ever-silent Khaddafy who would just watch or listen in the corner while Abu Sabaya laughed and boasted of his manhood.

"I will never forget those days," Marissa would later say.

One day she asked Abu Sabaya why he did it. The bandit said he had wanted to do it to one of the teachers. "But she was pregnant," he said.

She cursed him. He slapped her. She cried. He forced her to read the Qur'an. She read it. He slept. She could have killed Abu Sabaya then. When he came to her hut he would bring his guns. He would leave them in a corner while he slept.

Marissa wanted to kill Abu Sabaya, but she thought of the consequences. "What would happen to the other hostages?"

Later, much, much later, she asked Abu Sabaya if any of the children had been abused. The bandit told her "nobody among the children was raped."

"Maybe some were touched but not raped," he said.

THE HOSTAGES CRIED while Father Rhoel was being mauled. They heard him grunting and groaning.

It was the first time Mr. Rubio cried in all his life. He ran to the toilet and cried. The other hostages sat still, their heads bowed, tears in their eyes.

Every blow that hit the priest's body made the hair on their arms and the back of their necks stand up. It was eerie. It was ghoulish. The beating seemed endless. The women hostages on the other side of the hut prayed in silence.

"Please, enough," they pleaded. But the bandits refused to heed them.

Finally, when the bandits grew tired of hitting the priest, they pushed him down the hole of the roof. The other hostages caught the priest and laid him on the floor. He turned his body and hid his face and lay down on his side facing the wall. He was trembling all over, but he did not ask for help. He did not complain.

The bandits peered down on the hostages, smiling.

Father Rhoel's face was almost unrecognizable. Blood ran down his cheek on to the floor; it came from his bleeding nose and lips. His mouth did not stop quivering. The smell of blood, urine, and feces permeated the air. There were tears in his eyes but he was not crying.

The other hostages watched the young missionary. They wanted to help him, even embrace the man of God, but they too were afraid for their lives. They did not want to catch the attention of the bandits. It took almost half an hour before Nelson, a Catholic lay minister, approached him. He murmured some prayers, raising his hands over Father Rhoel.

Nelson removed the priest's bloodied and soiled clothes. Mr. Rubio removed his pants and underwear. Father Rhoel was black and blue all over. The other hostages brought water from the toilet and washed him.

From above, Abu Jandal called out. "Give him this," he said, as he threw down some tablets. "That will help prevent the swelling," he said. "Next time don't pray out loud or you will suffer the same fate," Jandal warned the hostages.

But the pain the bandits inflicted on Father Rhoel only seemed to push the young missionary to pray more intensely. The other hostages would later recount how, even as he trembled in pain, the priest never stopped praying.

Even in his sleep Father Rhoel prayed. Mr. Rubio, who slept beside the priest the whole time they were in the mountain, would later say that he heard the priest pray even in the middle of the night. He would pray for the other hostages, for his family, for friends and acquaintances.

AFTER FATHER RHOEL'S MAULING, the hostages were always on their guard. They tried not to offend the bandits. They became nervous and edgy. The bandits, too, avoided the hostages. They tried to distance themselves, except from the children.

The hostages could hardly sleep; they spent entire days thinking about what they would do if they got out of the mountain alive.

In the afternoon of the day the priest was beaten up, a bandit slapped Lydda in the face because she was handing biscuits out to the children. The bandit told her to give everything to the children.

"I'm trying to distribute it equally so that we will have something in the coming days," she said.

"You have no right deciding for anything here," the bandit said and slapped her.

The bandits spoiled the children. They did not want to see them crying or looking sad. When the teachers told the children to behave, the bandits got angry.

The Abu Sayyaf members were not actually a scary lot. They were as ordinary looking as most teenage boys, except that they carried their firearms carelessly and fired them indiscriminately. They wore ordinary shirts and pants.

They were, however, a suspicious lot. When the hostages prayed openly, they thought it was out of disrespect for them. Father Rhoel, along with the male hostages, used to pray the rosary aloud in the morning and in the afternoon. At first the guards allowed them. They did not mind. At least three of them were actually half-Christians. They were replaced later, however, by more radical guards.

THE ONLY THINGS that kept the hostages' sanity intact were hope and prayer, and elementary rituals. They counted the sunrises and sunsets, the times they were ordered out of their hut, the number of their companions who got sick.

Counting the rising and setting of the sun became a ritual for the hostages. A hand-drawn calendar on the wall of the hut, with every passing day crossed out, became their source of hope. Someday, somehow, the count will stop, they must have thought.

The children drew on the wall, in red and blue ink, memories of their homes and of classes in their schools. There was a hut that leaned on one side; a schoolbuilding with a flagpole that looked like a rocket ship ready for launch; rows of cabbages with stickmen watering plants; moon, sun and stars; kites and birds and an oversized ant.

The cheerful pictures pasted on the wall might have reminded them of the world beyond, of Zamboanga where they went to buy new pairs of shoes for graduation, of the basketball court in the village where they shouted their hearts out to cheer for their team, of the village church where they spent early mornings for dawn masses during Christmas.

The drawings and sketches on the wall of their mountaintop prison was their link to the world beyond the forest.

ON RADIO, Abu Sabaya threatened to start beheading the male hostages if the government failed to send movie star Robin Padilla, a Muslim convert, as chief negotiator. Among those to be beheaded were the priest, six teachers, and two students. The bandits also demanded that a representative from the Vatican join the negotiations.

The next day, the government negotiating panel composed of National Security Adviser Alexander Aguirre, Claretian priest Nestor Banga, a group of *ulamas* (Muslim religious leaders), and movie actor Padilla trekked toward the meeting place set by the Abu Sayyaf in the mountains of Upper Mahayahay, Maluso town, a three-hour hike from Camp Abdurazzak.

While walking to the mountains, Father Nestor, a native of Maluso, remembered that it was in Upper Mahayahay where a massacre occurred a few years back. The Abu Sayyaf killed a group of hunters for the simple reason that they were Christians.

It was Christmas eve 1994, and Ronaldo and Donato Ruda, Richard Pelaez, and Restituto Balansag were waiting for the lanky Claretian priest Alex Gobrin. The priest promised to visit the community in Lower Mahayahay and celebrate Midnight Mass there. He also said he would come early to join the hunters.

The priest was late, however. He was still nowhere in sight when the hunters decided to leave. The hunters left in the morning.

When they were in the mountains of Upper Mahayahay, they learned that someone somewhere in the forest had caught a wild pig earlier in the day. They decided to buy the pig instead.

On their way home, however, the group got lost and ended up in the hands of the bandits. They were brought deep into the mountain, hogtied, made to stand in line, and then hacked one by one.

The first one beheaded was Restituto Balansag. He died instantly. Only a small piece of skin connected his head to his body, which rolled down the slope of the hill. Next in line was Richard Pelaez. He looked straight into his young brother-in-law's eyes. Donato looked back. They were both afraid. As a bandit was about to strike down Richard, Donato shouted: "Let me die first."

The bodies rolled down the slope. The bandits all left, thinking everyone was dead. Donato survived. His thick jacket, which was used to blindfold him, had saved his life. The jacket covered his neck, blunting the bandit's bolo. After his rescue, he left Basilan for good. His father, however, refused to abandon their land in Lower Mahayahay.

"Almost 20 members of my family have died since the war erupted in the 1970s, but we stayed," Donato's father said. "It is part of life to die. We do not blame God. We offer our lives here and live in a faraway place. But we see the face of God in all the challenges that we encounter. The priests could leave and the Church, but we will remain until the last ounce of our strength, because God will not abandon us. Our faith did not waver despite the death of our family members. We have seen death in the face."

BEGINNING IN MAY 2000, after Father Rhoel was found dead and most of the hostages were rescued, news stories circulated that the bandits had tortured Father Rhoel and removed his nails while he was in Camp Abdurazzak. Most of the hostages, however, said they never saw or heard the priest being tortured. He was beaten up. He was spit upon. He was humiliated. He was made to suffer the fate of martyrs. But they maintained that he had not been tortured.

The bandits even quarreled among themselves on the afternoon of the day they assaulted Father Rhoel. It was the same afternoon a bandit slapped Lydda over an argument about the distribution of biscuits.

There was a change of guard at around three in the afternoon. Abu Jandal, the friendly bandit, was resting inside his bunker, watching Kipyong, the hostage who had become his friend, playing with the other children. Because of Abu Jandal, Kipyong had learned to pray with the bandits and perform their rituals.

That day he saw the guards gesticulating at Kipyong. "What are they doing?" Abu Jandal must have wondered.

When Kipyong passed by Abu Jandal's bunker, the bandit asked him where he was going.

"I'm getting water for the new guards. They're going to wash. It's prayer time already," the boy said. It is part of Muslim religious ritual to cleanse one's body before praying to Allah.

"Don't do it," Abu Jandal said. "You're supposed to fetch water only for the hostages, not for the guards," he said. "That was Daf"s order." He meant Khaddafy Janjalani, their leader.

Kipyong obliged and sat beside Abu Jandal.

The other bandits, seeing the boy sit down, shouted at him. "Come here!" Kipyong got up and ran toward the man. "You, lazy!" The man said, and hit the boy.

Abu Jandal came running. He carried a stick, which he used to hit the bandit who had punched Kipyong. The boy ran and went inside the hostages' hut. He saw Father Rhoel lying on the floor, trembling. The boy sat in a corner and waited for something to happen.

"Is Kipyong there?" It was Abu Jandal, peering down from the hole above.

"He's here," answered one of the hostages.

"Just relax, all of you," the bandit said. "Kipyong, are you all right?"

"Yes," Kipyong said, looking up. He saw a shadow behind Abu Jandal. "Abu, watch out," he shouted. But he was too late. One of the new guards hit Abu Jandal. The latter grabbed a gun, and pointed it at his attacker. His attacker grabbed it. They grappled on the roof of the hut.

"Run! Into the toilet," the women on the other side of the hut panicked. They were afraid the gun might explode and hit them. The men also went to the corners. "It's better to be safe," one of them said.

Outside, there was pandemonium. There was a lot of shouting in various languages. The hostages inside the hut did not know what to do. They rushed from corner to corner, trying to avoid getting hit by the increasingly imminent burst of fire. They did not know where to hide.

CHAPTER 6

THE RUSTLING OF LEAVES broke the silence. The bandits were moving around camp. "*Bangon* (Wake up)," they whispered. "Wake up. Everybody wake up," they ordered.

It was April 28, around ten in the evening. The women hostages had just gone to sleep inside the bunkers with the children.

"Get ready. Don't make any noise and cooperate," they ordered in low voices. "We are releasing all of you," the bandits assured the hostages. "Everybody will be leaving the camp."

No flashlights, they were told, as the hostages hurriedly stuffed whatever belongings they had at hand into plastic bags.

Sinangkapan teachers Lydda Ajon and Teresita Academia, who was pregnant, held on to each other. They were in the corner of the bunker when the bandits ushered the children out. When their turn came to leave the bunker and walk into the night, they could not find the other hostages. The men and the children were gone. Fear overtook them.

"Where are they?" Teresita asked.

"Move on," a bandit pushed the two from behind. They were led up to the "high ground" where the Abu Sayyaf leaders were staying.

Then Lydda saw Kipyong walking behind her. "Where are they? Where's your uncle?" The boy had stayed with her husband Rosebert, like the other male hostages, inside the hut during the bombings.

ESCAPE INTO THE UNKNOWN

"Uncle is at the back," Kipyong said. "He's with Father Rhoel and Mr. Rubio." During their captivity, the children had taken to calling the grown-ups aunts and uncles.

Once everyone reached the "high ground," Abu Sabaya spoke to the hostages. "We're leaving camp. The military has started the assault. Thousands of bombs will be dropped on us. We have to move out." Sabaya was speaking in an unusually mild way. It was the first time Lydda heard Sabaya speak without shouting.

The bandits ordered the hostages to form a long column. Father Rhoel was made to stand ahead of the others. A rope was tied around his waist and he was handed a 50-caliber machine gun to carry on his shoulder.

The other hostages carried bags, bullets, cannon shells, even guns. Mr. Rubio carried two heavy knapsacks. Even the children were made to carry B-57 shells which were too heavy for them. Some complained, but all were told to shut up.

Marissa was given a live howitzer shell to carry. "I can't carry it. It's too heavy," she complained.

Upon hearing her, Father Rhoel spoke. "Let me carry it for her," the priest volunteered.

"Give it to him," a bandit near Marissa said.

Marissa approached the priest.

"Let me have it," the priest said, putting down the machine gun.

"Listen to me, Marissa," Father Rhoel whispered. "I've given the school keys to the daughter of Joy Reambonanza. Get it from her when you're back in Tumahubong, all the 14 keys. Take charge of the school," he said.

She nodded.

"Here, take my bag and I'll carry that bomb," the priest said.

Marissa took the bag. She was teary-eyed. She looked at her friend who had already endured so much. She knew he was bidding her goodbye.

Almost like a reflex, she remembered some of their moments together. She recalled how he removed a leech from her face one day when they had the chance to talk to each other before she was brought to the "high ground." She remembered how the priest told her weeks ago that his lips were wounded because he drank from a torn can. She remembered how he called on her one night to ask if she had medicine because he had an upset stomach. She remembered when he asked her to lend him a blanket because he had the chills. She remembered when he asked her once, half-jokingly, if she could lend him her toothbrush. She had just laughed him off.

On the Monday they were abducted by the Abu Sayyaf, the priest had given Marissa a letter. Father Rhoel knew of his impending transfer to another mission, so he thanked Marissa for their friendship. The two were very close, like brother and sister. He used to fetch Marissa from her house in front of the convent and they would walk to school together almost every morning.

In the bandits' camp, Marissa heard how Father Rhoel suffered when he tried to prevent the bandits from taking her to the "high ground." But it was only when she was brought back to where the other hostages were that she saw Father Rhoel's bruises. She saw the sadness and the pain in his eyes.

"What did they do to you?" she remembered asking.

"It was not what they did to me that saddens me, Marissa," the priest answered through the wall of the hut. "It is what they did to Nelson and Dante."

ON APRIL 19, thirty days after the abduction, the bandits informed the hostages that they were releasing Nelson Enriquez and Dante Uban as a "birthday gift" to President Joseph "Erap" Estrada.

The children were playing outside when the bandits brought the two out of the hut.

"Where are you bringing them?" the children asked the bandits. "We want to go with them."

"No, you stay," Abu Jandal said. "We will release them because they're too old already."

"Why are their hands tied?" Chary Vergara asked. She saw that both teachers were barefoot. Their clothes had also been left inside the hut.

"We're tying them so that they can't escape," another bandit named Abu Jaber told the children as he ordered them to get inside the hut.

"Let the children play," Khaddafy Janjalani shouted from one of the bunkers.

The children watched as Abu Jaber and Sayyaf tightened the ropes. Then the bandits led Nelson and Dante down the mountain through a path in the forest. The children continued playing.

Less than an hour later, Jaber and Sayyaf came back. They were very dirty. Sayyaf had mud on his shirt and pants while Jaber had blood all over his arms and body. They ordered Kipyong and Chary to fetch water from the spring.

"Why are you dirty? What did you do?" Chary asked.

"We butchered a cow," Jaber answered.

"Where are our teachers?" Kipyong asked.

"They're already there," Sayyaf answered, pointing to the forest.

The children did not say anything. They went down the mountain to a nearby spring. When they came back, they heard the other bandits talking to Jaber and Sayyaf, who were washing themselves.

"Where did you leave the bodies?" one young bandit asked.

"We buried them," Sayyaf said.

"And the heads?"

"Shut up!" Jaber snapped. "We're sending them to Erap." He glanced at Kipyong and Chary, who were walking toward them with the water.

The children did not immediately tell the other hostages what they had overheard. They were too afraid.

THE ATTACK STARTED on April 22, Black Saturday. Helicopters and Air Force planes dropped their loads while 105-mm howitzer shells rained on the mountain from nearby military artillery posts.

The already shaken hostages were confused. "Why are they hitting us?" Lydda asked her husband Rosebert. "If they will try to rescue us, we will all die."

"Shhh," Rosebert said. "Be strong. We will survive. Maybe they are already nearby." He did not know it then, but intermittent rains were slowing down the soldiers who were groping their way through the forest.

At around 1 am on April 23, Easter Sunday, artillery again began to pound Mount Punoh Mahadji, leaving huge craters throughout the Abu Sayyaf camp. In the darkness, the children were crying and shouting.

"Let us prepare for the worst," Mr. Rubio told the other hostages, as he hid himself in the corner.

"Come out, come out," the bandits called on the children and the women. "Get out of there and go inside the bunkers." But when the male hostages moved to get out of the hut, too, one of the commanders ordered the guards to lock the door. "Let the soldiers bomb and kill the men," he shouted.

"What are you doing?" Father Rhoel demanded.

The bombardment went on for days. Thinking that all the hostages were inside the hut, the military spared it from the bombs and targeted the bunkers instead, where, unknown to the Air Force pilots, the women and children were hiding. The women hugged the children. They were all crying.

By April 24, several of the Abu Sayyaf's advance posts and mini-camps at the foot of the mountain were overrun. The bandits telephoned a local radio station and threatened to behead five male hostages unless the military backed off.

(By this time, the Sulu unit of the Abu Sayyaf had made its daring raid on the Malaysian resort of Sipadan, kidnapping 22 tourists and resort staff.)

"Let them continue the operations," Abu Sabaya said over the radio. "All they will get are the heads of the hostages, including the priest." The hostages were still unharmed, he said, but he hinted that the women and children could be in danger.

"They have sacrificed the lives of the children and we will not beg them to stop attacking us," Sabaya said. "We are ready for the operations and we can fight for one, two, or three months straight. It all depends on the government."

During the prolonged assault, two helicopters dropped leaflets on the camp, calling on the Abu Sayyaf to surrender.

The next day, the bandits again called a local radio station and forced Father Rhoel to ask the government to stop the military assault. "You are bombing us and not the armed men who are holding us," the priest said. "We're dying of fright."

"We can't sleep, and we're running out of food because of the military operations. It seems to me that we're going to die not from bullets but from fear," he said, under coaching from the bandits. He asked that the government work for the hostages' release through "peaceful negotiations, not bombing."

But government forces pressed on for the final assault. At least three MG-520 attack helicopters and two OV-10 Bronco bombers continued to pound the bandits' position.

On the afternoon of April 30, the military finally captured Camp Abdurazzak.

The soldiers saw the hand-drawn calendar and the cheerful pictures that adorned the walls of the abandoned mountaintop prison. It had been home away from home for the seventeen children and eleven adults held by the bandits.

The dates on the calendar were crossed out from March 20 to April 15. What happened after that was a mystery to the soldiers.

On the muddy dirt floor lay slippers, shirts, pajamas, underwear, and blankets, probably left behind in the confusion of the bombings.

But there was no single bandit or hostage in sight. The camp, when captured, was already abandoned.

ON THE OTHER SIDE of the forest, troops led by members of a Civilian Armed Forces Geographical Unit pushed hard toward Mount Punoh Mahadji from the village of Tumahubong. They endured days of hunger as they followed the trail of the bandits toward Camp Abdurazzak, and came under heavy fire from Abu Sayyaf sympathizers.

"We walked for days without food. A lot of us were wounded," admitted Private Bendah [he requested the use of a pseudonym] of the Army's 32nd Infantry Battalion. Helicopters carrying ammunition and food could not find the soldiers. The soldiers' radio batteries were drained. There was no communication, so bombs and artillery fire also rained on the troops.

"There was no choice but to move forward," Bendah said. "We were afraid but we had no choice." Leeches sucked even their eyes, their skins were full of wounds, and their bullets were running out. They forced themselves to cross ice-cold rivers in the middle of the night and climb cliffs to gain ground. They had to make do with cigarettes to forget the hunger and the pain.

The day before the bandits made their escape from Camp Abdurazzak, Bendah's unit reached the foot of Mount Punoh Mahadji. Weary and wounded, they were happy to see other units already there, returning fire.

However, Bendah, a veteran of other military encounters, was shocked with what he saw. Many soldiers were wounded and lying on the wet ground. What unnerved Bendah were the dead. Some were slung on trees, others on the perimeter fence of the Abu Sayyaf camp. There were dead soldiers in the middle of the firing zone, brains splattered on the grass and bowels being eaten by wild pigs. They could not be recovered, because the bandits did not stop shooting.

"We can't do anything," one soldier told Bendah. "The Abu Sayyaf have a lot of bullets and they are in a superior position. We have been here for three days already."

"Where's the reinforcement?" Bendah asked.

"I don't know," the soldier answered. "Maybe they forgot us already."

On a transistor radio, the soldiers heard the news that at least 32 soldiers and militiamen had been killed and 60 others wounded since rescue operations started on April 22. Bendah started counting the dead and the wounded. "There's more than that," he said to himself.

Two days later, Bendah was one of the first soldiers to enter Camp Abdurazzak after the Army's Special Forces stormed the abandoned lair. Military helicopters carrying boxes of ice cream and instant noodles arrived. Generals and colonels from the military's Southern Command based in Zamboanga City arrived, too, accompanied by journalists.

Bendah, carrying two gallons of ice cream with his M-16 rifle slung on his shoulder, proudly posed in front of one of the television cameras. He was smiling, unmindful of the taunts and shouts of his comrades. "Ma, Pa, I'm alive," he whispered to the machine.

That night, during the six o'clock evening news, a family somewhere in the slums of Manila smiled back at Bendah on television. "He's alive. Your crazy son is still alive and he's having ice cream," Bendah's father told his wife.

WHEN THE BOMBING STARTED, Kipyong, who was scared to death of the explosions, decided to tell Mr. Rubio what he had seen and heard about Nelson and Dante. But they were already too afraid for their lives to talk about it. Even in the middle of the night, shells were exploding nearby. The children cried the whole night. The older ones cursed the military.

"They don't know what they're doing," Anabelle would say. It was no different inside the bunkers, which were dug into the ground. From outside they looked like an ordinary hut, but inside they were big enough to hide all the women and children. When a shell burst, the earth would shake and the hostages thought the walls would collapse on them.

There seemed no end to the air assault. Hardly anyone ate. The women were told to cook only in the evening so that the smoke could not be seen. One time, Marissa was cooking noodles outside while Chary was boiling water when a bomb exploded nearby. They were almost hit.

"See what your government is doing now? They don't care about you anymore," a bandit commented from behind a tree where he was hiding.

But the hostages did not lose hope. After some time, the explosions became routine. They would hear more than a hundred explosions in a day.

The Abu Sayyaf, too, seemed not to mind it anymore. They would pray and shout every time a bomb exploded.

Every now and then, a bandit would go to the women's bunker and report that many soldiers had been killed outside the camp because of the landmines. To prove it, he would then show off the military bags and uniforms he said they had taken from the dead soldiers. But even some of the bandits were nervous too. Some would cry even in front of the hostages.

A bandit who admitted he was one of those who kidnapped Father Loi Nacorda cried so hard and trembled in front of the hostages that another bandit pushed him hard. He fell to the ground.

"Why are you afraid? You have a gun while we don't have anything," one of the children asked.

"I just remembered what happened to us when we abducted Father Loi. I watched him pray to your God," the bandit said. "He was not afraid because he prayed." Then the bandit fell on his knees, bowed his head, and prayed. "*Allahu Akbar*," he chanted.

Another bomb exploded near the bunker. "Let us pray too," Anabelle urged the hostages.

WHEN THE ESCAPE from Camp Abdurazzak started, the night was still dark and the path down the mountain was slippery. Bandits and hostages alike slipped down the mountain.

Lydda walked with Teresita, who was very weak. There were times when they were the last ones in line, except for their guards who pushed them forward. They walked in a single file, a hostage followed by a bandit. There was no way anyone could escape. No one dared to.

They were already at the foot of the mountain early the next morning when the military stormed the camp.

For five days the hostages trudged through the forest, evading soldiers and enduring thirst, hunger, mental torture, and even the occasional punch or kick from a bandit. They were not allowed to talk. Those found talking were kicked or hit with the butt of a rifle. They crossed rivers infested with leeches, and climbed hills on stiff trails.

Lydda could not imagine that, only a month after her abduction, she was again in the forest, dying of fatigue and hunger and thirst.

On March 20, the day she and husband Rosebert were taken, she had brought two bottles of mineral water to the Sinangkapan Elementary School in Tuburan town where they were both teachers. Before she closed the door of their house, she made sure that her miniature Santo Niño and rosary were in her bag.

Lydda spent the day watching her pupils practice for their graduation. It was three o'clock in the afternoon when the couple decided to start home. She sent off eight of her fellow teachers who boarded a van, then she and Rosebert mounted their motorcycle.

A few meters from the school gate, she saw three armed men with M-14 rifles. They were blocking the couple's way. "Get off that bike," one of the men ordered. Rosebert did not yield, so they hit him with the butt of a rifle and knocked him off. Lydda tried to scream but nothing came out of her mouth. She was trembling. She heard a vehicle screech from behind. She turned around and saw the other teachers. "Help at last!" she thought.

It lasted only for an instant, because she saw at least 20 armed men appear from every corner of the school grounds. They were pointing their guns at the teachers. "Come with us," the armed men shouted.

They followed the bandits. Lydda held on to her bag. She slipped her hand inside and groped for her Santo Niño. "Lord, please take care of us," she prayed. They walked into the unknown, toward the mountain. For two days and two nights, they hiked in the middle of a dense forest, the bandits' guns constantly pointed at them. It was about ten o'clock in the morning of the third day when they reached Camp Abdurazzak and saw the other hostages.

In the camp, Lydda and Anabelle cooked meals for the hostages. Most of the time, however, Lydda would catch Anabelle sitting on a huge root of a tree, her hands inside her jacket pockets, deep in prayer. Inspired by the Claretian teacher, Lydda looked for what remained of her bag, which had been burned earlier. Her right foot scoured the ashes, but she could not find her Santo Niño and her rosary. For a moment she lost all hope, but

Anabelle's presence reminded her to pray from the heart. She used her fingers to pray the rosary.

Many times, while she was on the camp grounds, Lydda could see soldiers from afar trying to penetrate the camp. But they always failed because the bandits would shoot at them, and there were landmines around the area.

Now, after a month in Camp Abdurazzak, Lydda and the other hostages found themselves walking again, for miles at a time and in darkness. Lydda never felt so tired in her entire life. The hostages could rest only when dawn broke, when the bandits stopped the group for fear that soldiers would find them.

For five days there was no food. They would drink water from streams and murky rivers. They were always on the run, as if wild animals were chasing them. Several times, they passed through military detachments. During the first time, the hostages got ready to drop for cover, thinking that the soldiers would fire at them. But to the hostage's surprise the sentries just let them through.

"Faster, faster," a sentry would call on the bandits. "Faster before our commander wakes up." Most of the sentries, especially those assigned in the evening, were Muslim CAFGU militias or MNLF integrees.

ONE MORNING, during one of their stops, Mr. Rubio, who was lagging behind the column, passed by Father Rhoel sitting on a protruding root. The priest had only Abu Said to guard him, while the school principal had four to help him walk.

The priest looked at the school principal straight in the eye and pointed to his left foot. Mr. Rubio saw that the priest's toenails were missing.

"Move on, move on," the guard pushed the school principal. The soles of his feet were scraped off and the pain was excruciating. He could not walk straight. The bandits kicked him from behind. "Old man, walk faster," they prodded him.

There is no way I can survive this ordeal, Mr. Rubio thought to himself. He was ready to surrender, to die rather than continue walking. The march was torture enough. But they seemed to be going nowhere, there was no food, and they had had to drink whatever was available.

Once, when the bandits espied some soldiers in the area, the hostages were forced to run. Mr. Rubio fell into a ditch and just lay there. He pleaded with the bandits to end his suffering and just kill him.

"I cannot move. Please, kill me. Cut my head off, please. I want to die," he said. The bandits looked at each other. They looked around and they nodded. "Here, cut it clean right here," the school principal raised his head and offered his neck.

"*Barong, barong,*" a bandit called out for a big bolo. "Sir, we'll do this for you," one bandit said. "Pray now and be ready."

Mr. Rubio closed his eyes and prayed. He waited. The air was still and he could hear the birds chirping. Then he felt something on his neck. It was not sharp. He opened his eyes and saw a bandit pointing a rifle at his nape.

"Your skin is too thick for the bolo," a bandit who was sitting on a rock called down. "Shoot him now," he urged the one holding the gun.

"Use your gun, please. Just shoot me in the head," Mr. Rubio pleaded. "Shoot me now," he said as he again closed his eyes. He pictured the face of his wife and recalled the happy days they had with the children.

But the man did not shoot. Mr. Rubio felt the rifle being withdrawn. He opened his eyes and saw Khaddafy Janjalani looking down at him in the ditch. "What are you doing there, Sir?"

"The principal wants to die," one of the guards answered.

"Pull him up. He's old enough to be your grandfather," Khaddafy ordered. "Don't hurt him. You must always respect your elders. If he can't walk, you carry him," he said and turned to leave.

The bandits took turns carrying Mr. Rubio. He would hold on to one bandit on his left side and walk with the aid of a stick. It was hard and the pain did not ease. Other times he would forget about himself and think of the other hostages. He knew that he was at the tail end of the column, while Father Rhoel was always in front.

One time, Mr. Rubio noticed that the women were lagging too far behind. He could not hear them anymore. When he looked back, there was no sign of them. Then he heard one of the bandits ask: "Where's Jandal?" Another answered: "Maybe he's enjoying himself." Mr. Rubio was cut to the quick.

Then he saw another chance to die. They were climbing a steep hill when he fell down and could not move an inch off the ground. "Please push me off the cliff and just tell Khaddafy later that I fell off," he pleaded. "Have mercy on me, kill me now."

"You want to die again?" a bandit asked. He called on his companions and asked them to help him carry the old teacher. "Let us throw him down the cliff," the bandit said. They dragged him toward the edge. Mr. Rubio could see the rocks down below but he chose to look into the ocean and pray.

"Now," he urged his guards. "Push me now," he ordered as he closed his eyes. The guards pushed Mr. Rubio, but backwards, away from the cliff. The school principal fell back. When he opened his eyes, he saw his guards laughing.

"You're really a fool," the bandits said, dragging the old man down the hill, into the unknown.

THE SEARCH FOR DIALOGUE

AURELIANO LAPING, also known as *Kumander* Leleng, is a 51-year-old "Muslim killer." The son of *Kumander* Luis Laping, a Christian militia leader who waged war on Muslims in the 1,970s, *Kumander* Leleng is believed to have "powers" that render him invulnerable to bullets and bolos.

He and his brothers became Christian vigilantes when his father died in an attack on a Moro rebel camp near Mount Punoh Mahadji.

"*Adunay panahon nga makapatay ko og usa ka Muslim kada adlaw. Gusto nakong sundon ang lakang sa akong amahan ug buhion ang iyang mga pangandoy* (There was a time when I killed at least one Muslim everyday. I wanted to follow my father's footsteps and make his ideals live)."

Because he was a legend, *Kumander* Leleng attracted a lot of followers—Christians and Muslims. Authorities looked at him as a necessary evil, someone who could balance the forces in the island.

"The Muslims kill Christians like animals. They cut their heads and rape the women. They kidnap Christians and kill them even if the families of the victims pay ransom," he preached to his followers.

It hurt him, he said, to see Christians suffering in the hands of Muslims. "I wanted to help the Christians, so I dedicated my life to defending them," he would say later.

He vowed that for every one of his men killed by Muslims, he would kill at least ten Muslims—men, women, or children, innocent or not.

Both Muslims and Christians feared *Kumander* Leleng and his *anting-anting*. People learned to avoid him especially when he took off his shirt, put on a scarf over his head, and walked barefoot. That meant he was ready to kill.

Because of poverty, *Kumander* Leleng was not able to finish school. He was in Grade Four when he stopped and started helping his father feed the family. His father hunted wild pigs in the forest or fished off the shore of Maluso, while his mother tended a small piece of land.

He had thirteen siblings, all male. Six died when they were still young because there was nothing to feed them with. Seven reached adulthood but later fell to Muslim bandits.

When he was twelve years old, *Kumander* Leleng earned twenty centavos a day as a grass cutter. Sometimes he worked in a coconut plantation for P10 a day, or joined an illegal logging firm at a rate of thirty centavos per board foot.

"When I learned to work, my family was happy. I was able to bring rice and fish for the family and, sometimes, even biscuits for my young brothers. My mother would cry. When I asked her why, she would tell me it was tears of joy. I would cry too, watching my mother."

When martial law was declared in 1972, the family left Maluso. When they came back a few months later, the town was already occupied by the military. It was then that the bloody Christian vs. Muslim saga started.

"Christians visiting their farms would not be able to come back. They were either hacked to death or shot. The men were always beheaded and the women raped. Later, no Christian wanted to go to their farms anymore." The Muslims had occupied the land.

The military decided to organize militia groups like the Civilian Home Defense Force and the Barangay Self Defense Units. *Kumander* Leleng's father, Luis, commanded one such militia unit.

Even after martial law was lifted, *Kumander* Leleng continued his crusade. The Army left the island and the Marines replaced them. "The rebel camps were still standing. War was not yet over," he said.

He earned the respect of military officials on the island. Once, an official asked him if they could attack a rebel camp. A family had been kidnapped and there was news the bandits were staying in a rebel camp near Maluso.

"Sir, if you want to take over Camp Omar, let me lead the attack. I only need seven of your men and I will also bring seven of mine," he told the Marine commander.

"It is against regulations," the official said. "There should be more soldiers than militiamen."

But *Kumander* Leleng insisted. "Sir, I grew up in Maluso. Based on what I know, we can take the camp with only a few men." Camp Omar was where his father died.

The commander finally agreed. He sent eighteen soldiers while Leleng brought fourteen of his men.

The group crawled to the camp the whole night. When they were inside, *Kumander* Leleng crawled under a house. He saw a woman frying something in the kitchen. He could see her through the slats of the bamboo floor. When the woman saw him, she ran toward a small room to wake her husband. When the man reached for his firearm, *Kumander* Leleng fired. The man and his wife were killed instantly.

His men engaged the bandits. They peppered the houses with automatic fire. "This is *Kumander* Leleng," he shouted. "I am here to get you!" He attacked like a crazy animal. The shooting did not stop until the rebels abandoned their camp.

After they rescued the victims, *Kumander* Leleng ordered his men to gather the bodies of the dead and the wounded. He cut off the heads of both the dead and the wounded and put them in a sack. The next day, he brought the heads to town and presented them to military officials.

The soldiers were shocked. Why did you do it? they asked.

"I just wanted to prove [to you] that I really got the kidnappers," he said.

After the Camp Omar attack, *Kumander* Leleng received numerous death threats. They didn't faze him. "If a Christian is killed, I also kill. Many times, I make the first move," he later said.

ON VALENTINE'S DAY 1999, Mirriam "Dedet" Suacito, the inter-religious dialogue coordinator for the Prelature of Isabela, began wondering why the catechists from Tumahubong had not yet arrived when it was already past eight o'clock.

In the middle of the seminar, the bodies of the dead catechists started arriving at the seminar site. They had first been laid outside the village church, but now were being brought to Isabela for the funeral rites. The first body to arrive was that of the driver, *Manong* Emiliano, the man everyone respected. He was known to everybody and was not afraid of anything.

"Who could have done it?" she asked herself. The old man was friend to both Muslims and Christians. Every time he passed through Muslim areas, people greeted him. He was the missionaries' passport to rebel-infested areas. Dedet remembered a time when armed men suddenly appeared in the middle of the road just to greet the old man.

But in Basilan, violence against Church workers was nothing new. If it weren't the catechists from Tumahubong, it would have been some other Christian. It could have even been her.

Dedet was born in Basilan but went to Manila to study. She came back to the island to work for the Catholic Church. In the beginning, it was just work, until she realized it was her "responsibility as a baptized Christian to serve the people of Basilan."

"It is not work, it is a mission. If I took my work only as a job, I would have left here a long time ago," she said. But the situation of the people of Basilan is a challenge to any Christian. "The people here are too poor, yet they continue to live here."

Claretian missionary Angel Calvo brought about Dedet's awakening. He brought her to a community of Muslims one day, sometime in the 1970s; she was shocked. There was no radio, no electricity, nothing.

She helped organized the Kapatagan Community Development program, which sought to return land to the Muslim people of Calvario village. It was an impoverished community struggling to survive amid many difficulties.

In her work she found meaning in her life as a Christian. "I was happy with my experience with the Yakans. There was no politics, only realities. The Muslims are sincere and true to themselves," she would say later.

There was so much to do. Too many people lost their own lands during the martial law years. There was an exodus of people because of the war.

The Claretians campaigned to return the land. The military did not appreciate it. It was the time when the church looked at the military as the personification of evil, Dedet said. "They spared no one. Muslims and Christians were their victims," Dedet said.

A young Muslim girl told her she had been raped. She cannot remember the girl's name anymore, but she cannot forget her tale. In measured words, the girl told her she was raped by a group of Christian vigilantes working as security guards at a plantation.

"I was really angry and it was then that I realized it was no joke to stand by one's faith," she said. "There was no idealism, it just came naturally. We were not forced to be religious nor forced to pray. I did not know how I learned to love the people, but maybe I was eaten up by my experiences—like seeing a Muslim farmer taken by a soldier on the mere suspicion of being a Muslim rebel."

It was not to court or convert the Muslims. "We don't talk about conversion. Those who speak about conversion are those who are outside the communities, those who don't understand the situation."

Dedet saw and heard it all—poor Muslims saying they were tired of war, tired of running around, seeking refuge in safer places only to be followed again by another war. They didn't want trouble, they said. In some areas, they armed themselves and ambushed rebels, who turned out to be· fellow Muslims. It was just too much for them.

ON AUGUST 21, 1985, at around 6:30 in the morning, a day before the fiesta of Maluso town, *Kumander* Leleng was playing cards in a friend's house near the church. Outside, the children were on their way to the town's Claret School, near the military checkpoint half a kilometer away, for the annual parade.

Suddenly, there was a burst of gunfire. *Kumander* Leleng ran outside, toward the checkpoint. He met men, women, and children running in the opposite direction. "The bandits have attacked," they shouted.

When he reached the school, *Kumander* Leleng saw that

it was already deserted. The firing continued. The militia leader looked for his children, but they were nowhere to be found. "Maybe they're just hiding," he said to himself. He went around to make sure his children were safe. Then the bandits saw him, and started shooting.

He looked back and saw a man aiming his rifle at him. *Kumander* Leleng ran to his house and took his Garand rifle. A bandit shot at him. He fired back. He put his rifle in the single mode and shot at anything that moved. The fighting dragged on.

He looked around for his men. They were not there. The soldiers were hiding too. Caught by surprise, most of them were just in their underwear; they had been taking a bath in a nearby stream when the bandits came.

Kumander Leleng asked a man hiding near his house to run to the town center and tell the police to bring reinforcements. The man came back with a lot of bullets, but no reinforcement. *Kumander* Leleng braced himself, and then started shooting. When he saw so much as a foot, he shot at it. When the body was exposed, he aimed to kill.

By eleven, the rebels were still there. Their number was growing. At around noon, *Kumander* Leleng was able to enter the military camp. The soldiers were not there. They were all hiding in the other corner of the camp. He shouted, "I am *Kumander* Leleng, your reinforcement."

At around one, *Kumander* Leleng's men from a nearby village finally arrived. He ordered them to secure the camp and recover the bodies of the bandits who had already died. The bandit leader, *Kumander* Mike, was already dead, his head all blown up.

Military helicopters flew in at around two. They bombed the surrounding areas, and it was only then that the bandits withdrew to the mountains. The people counted the dead bodies. All fourteen bandits who were killed bore holes in the head from *Kumander* Leleng's Garand.

The dead were brought to the town plaza for identification, but nobody claimed the bodies. *Kumander* Leleng dumped the bodies in a common grave. The next morning, he found that the bodies had been stolen in the middle of the night.

It has been said that *Kumander* Leleng killed all those men in just an hour. Legend has it that bullets bounced off his naked body, or that he was shooting the bandits as if he were shooting birds. People said the militia leader fought barefoot and naked.

But *Kumander* Leleng himself cannot imagine how it exactly happened.

"I don't know why they did not hit me," he would say later, adding that he was not even prepared when the bandits came.

After the incident, *Kumander* Leleng became even more popular among the people. "They would say that I have an *anting-anting*. It is true that I have something with me, but I believe it was God who took care of me. Maybe it was a miracle. I don't know. I have been to a lot of encounters, but it seems bullets just can't hit me. I have been in a lot of ambushes, but I have never been hit."

He said he was grateful to God. "I believe that He gave me an *anting-anting*. I always prayed before I went on an operation. I always asked God to guide me and make me safe because what I am doing is for the good of the Christian community," he said. "Thank God, we never had a lot of casualties, but we were able to bring home a number of Muslim heads."

IN 1984, on the road to Tumahubong, Claretian priest Eduardo Monge and Sister Heide of the Daughters of Charity were kidnapped. They had not been abducted for money. The kidnappers just wanted a mosque built in their community. When Bishop Jose Maria Querexeta promised to build a mosque, the kidnappers released the priest and the nun.

The kidnappings, however, have not stopped, and Muslims and Christians alike continue to be unwitting victims. It will take a long time before there is peace in the island, Dedet said. But she is not giving up.

"Each side sees the other as a threat, especially when Christians started arming themselves. The Muslims were afraid too, because Christians were also killing them."

"Many communities are already tired of war. They are very tired already. Some have decided to defend their communities so that no bad elements—Christians or Muslims—enter their area."

Taking up arms is not an option for Dedet. It is not the right answer to the conflict, she said. "Based on what I have seen, arming people does not solve the problem. It just muddles the issue."

After the death of Father Rhoel, Christian groups painted crosses all over the province to defy the Abu Sayyaf's demand to remove all the crosses from the island. They made a mistake, however, when they painted even the houses of Muslims.

"It was very insulting to the Muslims. Such an attitude sometimes makes it difficult for Muslims and Christians to enter into a dialogue."

"Hearing the stories of the kidnap victims, their traumatic ordeals, the anguish of the families of those who did not survive, can be very painful," Dedet said. She admitted that her prejudices against Muslims came back temporarily when Father Rhoel was killed. "There was a point when I wanted all the Abu Sayyaf killed," she said.

She recalled the fate of the sixteen Christians who were killed by the Abu Sayyaf during Father Nacorda's kidnapping. "They were killed not only because they were Christians but because they were poor," Dedet said.

These traumas brought people closer to the church, Dedet said. "Many Christians in the island have already seen the church as their only hope, their only safeguard amidst all the threats, even from poverty. Many feel that the church is their only refuge."

The Christians of Tumahubong are an example. Despite being one of the worst victims of the Abu Sayyaf, the church in Tumahubong has remained strong.

"Despite the many atrocities that have happened, the Claretians did not leave. Even amidst all the threats, they are there in the middle of their people, journeying with them, letting the faithful feel their presence," Dedet said.

Without the church in Basilan, there would be a mass exodus of Christians. "The church in Basilan is not only poor in material things but is living the evangelical [virtue of] poverty being preached by theologians."

She is optimistic that with enough patience, perseverance, and sincerity, a genuine Muslim-Christian dialogue will take root.

During such community dialogues, Muslims and Christians share their experiences. Once, a Muslim child narrated how, in the past, Christians had killed her parents, grandparents, and relatives.

Another time, a Christian teacher who had earlier been kidnapped vented her feelings. Another teacher, a Muslim, stood up and said he had also experienced discrimination, when the military refused to believe he was a teacher and accused him of being an Abu Sayyaf bandit. He was mauled, he said.

KUMANDER LELENG decided to put down his gun after Spanish Claretian missionary priest Father Eduardo Monge convinced him.

"*Kumander* Leleng, you have to change your life. You have become notorious to the Muslims on the island. It is time that you change," the priest told him.

"Father, I can change my life if my father would live again, if my brothers would come back to life, and the Christians who died in the hands of the Muslims would rise from their tombs," he answered.

"But what you are doing is against God and is against the law," the priest argued.

"Father, how can I change my life if the Muslims continue doing evil to my fellow Christians? We have been so oppressed, Father. Nobody would defend us. Let me be, Father, so that the Muslims will also feel what we feel. What they do to the Christians, I will do to them. If they kill, I will kill. If they kidnap, I will kidnap. If they rape, I will also rape, so that they will feel the pain that we have been feeling."

"*Kumander*, if only for the good of Basilan and out of respect for me, a priest, talking to you, please change your ways," Father Monge said.

"How?" *Kumander* Leleng replied, finally.

"Simple. Take the Bible. Read the Word of God."

"I don't have a Bible," the vigilante leader said.

"Tell me what kind of Bible you want. I will give it to you."

"But how do I listen to the Word of God?" *Kumander* Leleng asked.

"To read the Bible, you must concentrate and feel the Word of God in your heart. Then you will hear. It would be better for you to read early in the morning or in the evening."

"Can I depend on the Bible?"

"Yes."

Kumander Leleng accepted the challenge and studied the Bible after the priest returned with a new Visayan edition.

During the first night, the Muslim killer flipped through the pages. "I read deep into the night with only a flickering lamp as light," he later said. "I don't know why when I first opened it, it opened on the page where the Ten Commandments were. I trembled when I read it, because I had committed all the sins mentioned there."

He knelt on the floor and asked God for forgiveness. "Lord, forgive me for I have done all these bad things. I will now change my life."

In the morning, he called all his followers. "We are already old. Let us change our ways. We must be always ready to fight and defend our faith. But if we ever kill, let it not be because of revenge and not just on any Muslim. Starting today, we will punish those who are guilty, Muslims or Christians, by implementing the laws of the land."

Most of his men followed his example. He himself became a local church leader in his village in Tubigan, Maluso. He also reconciled with the Muslims. He has more Muslim followers now than Christians. They have not converted to Christianity, but when *Kumander* Leleng leads the Sunday prayers in the chapel they go with him. He also goes to the mosque from time to time to meet the families of his followers.

"I believe that if we put into practice what the Bible says, even the Muslims would see our example," he said.

One day, a young Abu Sayyaf member told him that their leaders had taught them that if they killed a Christian or died fighting the Christians, they would ride on a white horse to heaven when they die.

Leleng told the boy: "If you do bad things and kill innocent people, you will never go to heaven. You are going to jail because I will put you there myself."

"Life is short," *Kumander* Leleng said. "I have a few years in this world to live. So what do I do? I want to work for peace now with the Muslims. Before I go, I want to leave a story. I would want to let the world know that once there was a man named *Kumander* Leleng. He was a bad man, but he later changed his ways and made his town peaceful, he helped Muslims and Christians work together."

"If someday, another conflict erupts, my prayer is that they will remember the good I have done and not do the bad things that I did," said *Kumander* Leleng, the man now better known as Aureliano Laping, Vice Mayor of Maluso.

CHAPTER 7

FOR FOUR DAYS AND FIVE NIGHTS they walked, without eating. They forged their way downhill and then up again, avoiding the sharp rocks and the open roots. They marched in the dark, the rough stones cutting into their feet, the thorns penetrating their clothes, the mosquitoes and leeches feasting on their blood.

DEATH IN THE OPEN

They rested during the day, to avoid being spotted by pursuing soldiers, and they marched the whole night, as though wild animals were chasing them.

"*Lakad, Father, lakad, malapit nang dumating ang pahinga* (Walk, Father, walk. Rest will come soon)," a bandit prodded Father Rhoel from behind as someone else tugged on the rope that was tied around his waist.

Then one of the bandits signaled everybody to stop. The children—tired, sleepy, and wet—wasted no time and dropped to the ground. The older ones moved more slowly, reclining on tree trunks. Even the bandits, hungry and muddy as the rest, were weary. All were wet from the dew and from last night's rain. There seemed to be no stopping the rain in the forest.

After a few minutes, Ustadz Nur, the bandits' "operations officer," ordered everybody to stand up. "We have to move before they come nearer," he said. Ustadz Nur had been a public school teacher in Basilan before he joined the Abu Sayyaf.

"Do you know what you're doing?" Abu Amira, the medic, asked, within earshot of Mr. Rubio and other hostages. "Everybody's tired and we're not getting anywhere. Where are we heading, anyway?"

"Shut up, Amira," Ustadz Nur answered angrily. "I know what I'm doing."

"If I only knew beforehand that we would just walk around and around the forest, I would have not joined this operation," Abu Amira complained. "Abu Hasser and I could have asked Khaddafy for a vacation." Abu Hasser was Abu Amira's younger brother.

"We're useless in this operation," the teenage Abu Hasser murmured. "We're medics and there are no sick people here."

"Do you really have plans for us?" Abu Amira confronted Ustadz Nur. "You're just getting us killed."

"Shut up, the two of you!" Ustadz Nur shouted. "Just get up and walk."

The stragglers resumed marching. It was Wednesday, May 3.

At around 6 a.m., Ustadz Nur decided to stop. The hostages lay down on the wet grass, ready for a long rest. The day was starting to turn bright, the sun's rays beginning to penetrate the damp forest.

They had rested for barely 15 minutes when one of the bandits came running back from the front, ordering everybody to move back. "Slowly, move back. Don't stand up, just move back," he ordered in a low voice, almost whispering.

"Something must be wrong," thought Mr. Rubio, who was toying with a stick. "The military must be nearby," he whispered to Rodolfo Irong, a teacher from Sinangkapan Elementary School, who was sitting beside him. They retreated slowly until they felt their backs pressing against the trunk of a mango tree. Both closed their eyes, resting and thinking of their ordeal.

It had been exactly forty-five days since they were kidnapped by the Abu Sayyaf.

Several times during their stay in Mount Punoh Mahadji, the male hostages talked about escaping, especially when they heard from the children that the bandits were planning to hack the older men to death. But they changed their mind after teacher Rosebert refused to join them. "I can't come with you," Rosebert said. "My wife Lydda is here and I don't want to leave her behind." Nobody argued with him.

Another time they heard rumors that the teachers would be released. Excitement filled them, but their joy was short-lived, after Father Rhoel talked to the bandits and pleaded for the release of the children instead. The priest also insisted that if ever the Abu Sayyaf released the hostages, he would go last. He was a priest, he said, and he had nothing to lose.

"I will never forget him," Mr. Irong said to Mr. Rubio once.

"Who?" asked Mr. Rubio.

"Your friend, the priest," Mr. Irong answered. "He's something."

In their six weeks on the mountain, everybody noticed how Father Rhoel spent his time praying. Most of the time, he prayed alone and fervently. Nobody heard the priest complain. At times, he even skipped his food and gave it to the children. And he was always optimistic, confident that everything would turn out fine.

AT AROUND EIGHT IN THE MORNING, the bandits ordered everybody to stand up and start walking again. Lydda observed that they were already out of the forest. She could see that they were in a coconut plantation; she saw a lot of gmelina, lawaan, and mango trees.

Their guards, however, kept moving back and forth. They would order the hostages to move forward, but after a few minutes they would come back and tell them to retrace their steps. "Are we lost?" Lydda asked her husband Rosebert.

At around 8:30, the bandits again let the hostages rest and gave them young coconuts for breakfast. Bananas were also distributed, and the children devoured it in their hunger.

After eating, the group moved again. They moved from one place to another, from one hill to the next. They did this the whole morning, walking as if in circles, until they reached a slope where there was a lot of coconut trees and some kind of shrub that grew tall but had a lot of thorns. Nearby a creek was flowing, a treat for the thirsty hostages.

Mr. Rubio saw Abu Sabaya use a cellular phone. "If this takes longer, it might be difficult for us to leave Basilan," he heard the bandit telling someone on the other end of the line.

Five hostages—Father Rhoel, Ruben Democrito, Mr. Rubio, Rosebert, and Lydda—sat together around a small tree with thorns. By then it was already noon, and the hostages distributed small balls of rice and slices of cooked string beans to each hostage. The children swallowed everything and satisfied their thirst at a nearby spring. The older hostages, however, were not allowed to stand up. Instead, the bandits told the children to fetch water for their teachers.

After eating, the male hostages were bound together in twos. When a bandit approached Mr. Rubio, the school principal offered his right hand, thinking that, whatever happened, he could still use his left, which the bandits allowed free because "the old man had a hard time walking."

The bandits tied Mr. Rubio back to back with Mr. Irong, both of whose arms were bound. Father Rhoel was paired with Ruben, while Rosebert was roped to a B-57 shell and then moved to the upper slope with his wife.

Lydda sat under a tree while her husband lay on the ground beside her. The bandits rested on the lower slope a few meters below Father Rhoel, Ruben, Mr. Rubio, and Mr. Irong.

Everyone tried to get some rest—except the children, who enjoyed playing with the younger bandits. Some of the younger Abu Sayyaf climbed the coconut trees and tossed the coconuts down to the children, who in turn distributed it to everyone else.

Khaddafy Janjalani, Abu Sabaya, and the other Abu Sayyaf leaders sat nearby, talking earnestly. Abu Jandal bathed himself in the nearby creek, while Abu Jar, Abu Bilog, Abu Hapsin, and Abu Mahamdi exchanged jokes with the children.

After eating the coconuts and drinking its water, the teachers and some of the bandits lay down to sleep; the children continued playing.

Lydda watched Father Rhoel, Ruben, Mr. Rubio, and Mr. Irong trying to catch the shade of the shrub. As the heat rose, the four men tried to adjust themselves to avoid the sun. Lydda smiled to herself. "These old men are acting like children," she thought.

By two in the afternoon, Mr. Irong, who was wearing two sweatshirts, could not stand it anymore. He called Kipyong and Ryan Laputan, another of the children-hostages, and asked them to loosen his knot so that he could remove his shirt. The guards were just a few meters away, but they were not watching.

"Why did you tie them up?" Lydda asked a bandit who was sitting nearby.

"We don't want them to escape," he said.

"Why didn't you tie us up too?" she asked, just to make conversation. Her husband seemed to be already asleep beside her.

"You don't know where to go," the bandit said.

Nearby, Anabelle told Chary not to go too far. "Don't leave Cristy and Romela," she said. "Také care of them, *ha*, Chary?" Anabelle was sitting with her sister Romela nearby.

"Yes, auntie," Chary answered, nodding her head. She was sitting on the grass with her younger sister, Cristy, sleeping on her lap.

Father Rhoel turned his head. "Don't leave each other," he told them. "Whatever happens, always stay together."

"Chary, you take care of your sister. Don't be afraid," the priest said. "When we get back home, I will bring all of you to Jollibee in Zamboanga. We will have hamburger," he promised, smiling.

Abu Jaber and Abu Mahamdi went near Chary.

"You leave the children alone," Anabelle warned. "They won't bother you."

"Where are we going?" Chary asked Abu Mahamdi, who had already become her friend.

"We're going to Sulu. A boat is waiting for us on the beach," the bandit answered.

"I don't want to go to Sulu," Cristy said, opening her eyes.

"Don't worry, Cristy. We will release you there and you can go home to your families," Abu Jaber assured her.

"SOLDIERS, THE SOLDIERS are here!" the bathing Abu Jandal shouted from the creek below. "They're in the cassava plantation," he shouted.

It was around 3:30 in the afternoon.

"Enemies!" Abu Jandal shouted. "The enemies are here!"

Lydda, who was about to close her eyes, sat still. With Ruben tied behind him, Father Rhoel looked around but did not move. The children stopped playing and immediately sat on the ground.

"When the shooting starts, just drop to the ground," the priest shouted at the children.

The bandits roared in laughter. Some were still standing, calling on the children to come back and play. Some lay on the ground, while others sat, caressing their rifles. Khaddafy Janjalani, Abu Sabaya, and the other leaders continued talking, ignoring Abu Jandal.

The children saw Abu Jandal running toward them without his shirt on. The other bandits laughed and pointed at him. The children joined in the laughter.

"Nobody move! Drop to the ground!" someone shouted from somewhere. Bursts of automatic gunfire followed and filled the air.

"We're soldiers! Drop to the ground!"

"Don't shoot! Don't shoot! We are hostages! We are hostages!" Chary shouted at the top of her voice.

"Shout!" Chary heard Anabelle urging her. "Shout, Chary, shout!"

Lydda saw her husband hit in the first volley of fire. He had not been able to move because one of his arms was tied to the big B-57 shell. She lunged faced down to the ground. When she looked up, Lydda saw the soldiers. But two Abu Sayyaf bandits came near her, aiming their guns at her husband.

"No!" she shouted, as loudly as she could. "Don't shoot my husband, please." But the bandits didn't hear her in the din of the firefight.

She saw blood oozing from Rosebert's body. She crawled toward him and untied his arms. He was grimacing in pain. Then Lydda felt something dig into the flesh of her left arm. It immediately went numb, but she managed to drag her husband to a nearby thicket. Bullets were flying all around; Lydda lost track of where they were coming from. She just wanted to hide with her wounded husband.

Chary saw that her sister Cristy had been hit. She turned her head for help, when she saw something flash and blood spurt from Anabelle's head. The teacher fell. Her sister, Romela, was crying by her side. Sinangkapan teacher Mrs. Editha Lumame was bleeding nearby; she was also crying.

The young girl saw the bandits run for safety, even leaving behind an M-14 and a Baby Armalite rifle. She wanted to take the guns but she saw her friends Abu Bilog and Abu Hapsin nearby. The two Visayans had told her earlier that they had joined the Abu Sayyaf because they could not find work.

"Chary, go! Escape now!" Abu Hapsin shouted at her.

She started crawling and moved past Father Rhoel. She saw that the priest had been hit; there was blood on his shirt. He was still alive, but he was not moving. Ruben Democrito, however, had a hole in his head. "He's dead," she thought.

She saw Abu Jandal next, running up from the creek toward her. When she turned to take cover and hide from the bandit, she saw Abu Ben, one of Father Rhoel's guards, hit in the buttocks. He tried to recover his gun, but could not come near it because of the gunfire. Abu Ben crawled downhill toward the other bandits.

When the shooting started, Mr. Rubio actually thought he, Mr. Irong, Father Rhoel, and Ruben were perfectly safe. There was a rock just above them and the ground was low. The place was a natural foxhole. Even if the soldiers and the bandits exchanged gunfire, the four of them, who were in the middle, would have been safe if they just lay close to the ground.

The military attacked from the higher ground, from the slope where Rosebert and Lydda were, while the bandits were on the other side, on the lower ground.

When he heard the firing, Mr. Rubio saw the bandits run. The bullets came from both sides. At the first burst, Mr. Rubio tried to untie himself while lying down. He turned to his side. There was a loud explosion from a B-57 rocket. A splinter hit him in his left armpit.

He dropped on the ground and shouted to his companions to crawl. Mr. Irong immediately crawled toward the upper ground where Lydda and Rosebert were. Kipyong and Ryan having earlier loosened the rope that bound the teachers, it was easy for both of them to move.

"Let's escape," Mr. Irong said. He stood up and ran to one side, toward the soldiers Lydda had seen earlier.

Mr. Rubio was down on his stomach, facing the higher ground. He looked back at Father Rhoel and Ruben. He saw the two move, stand up, and jump over a thicket in the direction of the bandits on the lower ground. They were not able to go around the tree where the four of them were sitting because of the vines and thorns. If they had wanted to move toward higher ground, they would have had to go around the bush and run uphill toward the military.

The school principal thought the priest and the teacher jumped to hide on the other side of the tree. But even in the pandemonium, he knew Father Rhoel and Ruben could not move toward the higher ground. "They will have a hard time," Mr. Rubio thought. That was the last time he saw Father Rhoel and Ruben.

Mr. Rubio saw Anabelle. She was already dead. He saw the children crawling uphill. He could hear Chary shouting.

"We are hostages," Chary shouted again and again as she crawled toward the soldiers. The other children followed her. She moved past Lydda, who was crying beside her husband.

"Ma'am, Sir, we'll go ahead," Chary told the teacher.

"Go on, look for the military," Lydda pushed Chary and the other children.

"Help us, we are hostages," Chary shouted in the direction of a soldier she saw taking cover behind a nearby tree.

Mr. Rubio saw the bloodied body of Editha Lumame near 12-year-old Emelyn Cachuela, who was breathing deeply. He wanted to turn back but his body refused to move. He felt weak. It was then that he realized he was wounded too. It was painful for him to inhale. He went on crawling uphill. Finally, he reached Chary, Cristy, Kipyong, and Marissa.

"Sir, my sister is wounded," Chary said, pointing to Cristy. Mr. Rubio saw the blood.

"I'm sorry, I cannot carry her. I have no strength anymore. Just crawl," he said.

"Sir, I'm thirsty," Cristy was crying. "Please, sir, give me water."

"No. Just crawl, all of you," Mr. Rubio said. "Chary, look for something to tie your sister's arm," he ordered.

Chary left and then came back. She handed the school principal a piece of cloth. He tied Cristy's arm.

Then Kipyong carried Cristy.

The firing continued.

A soldier grabbed Chary's shirt and dragged her to safety. She looked around and saw Kipyong carrying her sister. Marissa was crawling beside them. They went inside a nearby hut.

"Out! Out!" a soldier called to them. "To the cassava plantation," he shouted.

The fighting went on.

Chary thought lightning and thunder were hitting them from all sides. Running toward the cassava plantation, she saw the wounded Emelyn, crying. Chary crawled back to get her friend, but a soldier grabbed her and carried her into the middle of the cassava plantation. There she saw Marissa, Kipyong, and Cristy.

Chary cried as she wiped the blood off her sister's arm.

Mr. Rubio saw that the soldiers who were withdrawing toward the cassava plantation already had some children with them. Abu Sayyaf bandits were running here and there, shooting at the soldiers and the children.

The school principal lay down on the ground and closed his eyes. He could no longer move. He heard three bandits come near him.

"Let us kill this one," one said.

Mr. Rubio prayed and prepared himself.

"No, let us come back for this one later," another said.

"Leave him, he can no longer walk," the other said.

Another volley of fire came from the soldiers. The three bandits scampered in different directions. Mr. Rubio hid under a bush. He could hear Lydda and Rosebert talking to each other.

"Bap, don't leave me, Bap," Lydda cried, holding her husband's hand.

"Dang, don't despair. Live, Dang. *Animo lang*, Dang," Rosebert answered.

They had been crawling toward the soldiers, but they had already lost a lot of blood and were too tired.

A soldier came near them when the children were rescued.

"Those who are not wounded, drink," they heard a soldier tell the children. "Those who are wounded, don't drink."

Lydda and Rosebert continued crawling for a few more meters. But they were too tired. The couple lay still. Then they heard voices again.

"Dang, the soldiers are back," Rosebert said. "We will live."

They listened.

"Don't move yet," Rosebert said. "Let us make sure that they are not bandits."

Then silence. The moving sounds stopped. The shooting stopped. When Lydda looked at her husband, Rosebert did not move.

"Bap, speak to me, Bap," Lydda shook her husband.

"I can't do it, Dang," he whispered.

"Let us pray," she urged her husband.

He did not answer. She cried. "If we die, we die together," she sobbed.

"Nobody dies together at the same time," Rosebert joked even as he gasped for breath. They held each other's hands.

"Dang, I can't take it anymore," he said.

"No, no, please!" she cried.

Then he was silent. Lydda held on to his hand tightly.

"Dang, look at the birds," he said.

Lydda heard the helicopters coming.

Then they heard a man's voice.

"There are more dead here. I think these two are dead."

Lydda tilted her head and saw a soldier examining the bodies on the ground. Before she passed out, she managed to croak, "We're not dead. We're still alive."

MR. RUBIO was planning to hide under the thicket until it was safe. He saw some bandits pass behind him. Later, the soldiers came back. "Secure the area, secure the area," a soldier shouted. Mr. Rubio remained where he was. "Maybe I will die here," he thought. But he saw no blood on his clothes. "I will live," he said to himself.

"Secure the area, secure the area," he heard the soldier again.

"I am safe. The military is here," Mr. Rubio thought.

"Sarge, I'm here. I am a hostage," the school principal shouted.

"Stand up," someone shouted back.

"I cannot stand," Mr. Rubio answered.

"Stand up," a soldier shouted angrily.

"I can't. I'm wounded. I'm Mr. Rubio, the principal."

"The principal is here," someone shouted.

Armed men pulled him out of his hiding place. But almost immediately Mr. Rubio's fear returned, when he heard a former bandit, who had been integrated into the military, talking to the soldiers.

"Sir, this is my uncle. Sir, he's my uncle. Sir, please, this man is my uncle," the former bandit, who knew Mr. Rubio from Lamitan, told a military officer three times. (Moros in Basilan call older men "uncle" as a sign of respect.)

While waiting for another helicopter to arrive and evacuate the dead and the wounded, the school principal sat near the soldiers who gave him first aid. Mr. Rubio saw that an officer, a young lieutenant, was fuming mad. He was cursing the soldiers around him.

Fresh troops arrived a few minutes later in two armored tanks. Immediately, the young lieutenant rushed toward the officer inside the newly arrived vehicles. The lieutenant was carrying an M-60 machine gun, which he threw inside the tank. He called a soldier inside the vehicle who was carrying a 50-caliber machine gun.

"Give me that," the young officer shouted, taking the soldier's machine gun. He put it on the ground and dismantled it. He then stood up and shouted at the officer inside the vehicle. "Why are you bringing a gun without a firing pin?" He also threw the 50-caliber machine gun inside the tank. "Throw all these. These are useless."

Then the helicopter arrived.

Mr. Rubio told the soldiers that Father Rhoel was hiding in the bushes.

AS THE HELICOPTERS LIFTED OFF from Mount Punoh Mahadji to bring the wounded to the hospital, villagers in Tumahubong held a procession to observe the feast day of San Vicente Ferrer, their patron saint. Unlike previous fiestas, it was a solemn affair.

Their children were still on the mountain, and their priest, they feared, was being tortured; he was nowhere near to carry the censer that burns the incense.

The faithful sang songs and recited the rosary as they walked slowly around the village, the saint's statue on the shoulders of four men, followed by the women and their flickering candles.

As the congregation made its way back to the church, the head of the statue suddenly fell over. Everyone gasped; the crowd shuddered. "It's an omen," an old woman said.

In Isabela, on the other side of the island, tears rolled down the cheeks of the blind woman Dolor. She had just seen another sign, another red mark, this time on the hands of Mr. Rubio's wife. "Let us pray," she told those beside her.

Three days later, Chief of Staff Angelo Reyes of the Armed Forces of the Philippines visited Mr. Rubio at the Infante Hospital in Isabela.

"How are you, Sir," the general asked Mr. Rubio.

"I'm fine, thank you," the school principal answered. "Where are the other hostages?"

"They're in the hospital in Zamboanga," General Reyes answered. "The priest was not fortunate."

Tears filled Mr. Rubio's eyes. It was only then that he realized the worst had happened. Father Rhoel had not made it.

CHAPTER 8

ON THURSDAY, MARCH 22, 2001, a year and two days after the Abu Sayyaf swooped down on the little village of Tumahubong, excitement was in the air. White gowns brightened the open windows of some of the nipa-thatched huts; the children who had missed last year's graduation ceremony were finally going to march.

THE END OF THE JOURNEY

Claret School's 24th commencement exercise was a year late, but now there was no stopping it. Two days before, word reached the people of Tumahubong that armed men were again poised to attack. This time, however, the villagers were not afraid.

"Welcome Back! Happy Anniversary!" the teachers wrote in jest on the blackboard at a first-floor entrance to the school.

The previous Tuesday, March 20, Claretian missionary priest Nestor Banga arrived in the village and celebrated Mass with the survivors of last year's attack. After the Mass, people greeted each other a "Happy Anniversary."

"O, *ano naman yon* (What was that all about)?" asked Father Edgar Zamudio, the new village priest.

"Oh, Father, we're just celebrating our first year of life from the hands of the Abu Sayyaf. Today's our birthday," said Joy Reambonanza, who was at the Mass with her two daughters. No rumor of an Abu Sayyaf attack could dampen her spirits.

AT THE CONVENT behind the San Vicente Ferrer Parish church, people had been busy even before the sun was up. They had taken over the priest's quarters and turned it into a big restaurant.

Manang Perla, the toothless, festive cook, was preparing a feast in the kitchen. A group of women was busy arranging rice cakes, buko salad, leche flan, and bread and cakes on a table in the sala under a huge picture of a smiling Father Rhoel.

Father Edgar's room had become an instant stockroom for cans of cooking oil, bottles of soy sauce and vinegar, boxes of pasta, sacks of rice and flour, plates, spoons and forks, and table knives—all borrowed from or donated by neighbors. Inside Father Rhoel's former room, a roasted pig and several dishes of fried chicken roosted on the floor.

The aroma of pepper, vegetables, sweet chili sauce, vinegar, and other seasonings mixed with the smoke from the firewood in the kitchen.

At the back of the convent, several men were butchering a pig. "It's fiesta time," shouted a group of teenage boys who were carrying a guitar.

"Don't just sing there, help us here," three girls shouted back as they tried to hold on to a chicken they were trying to kill.

"*Hoy*, is everybody all right? Where's the *tuba*? Don't start drinking *ha*," Manang Perla shouted at her husband from the kitchen door.

"It's a special day for the village, it's Tumahubong's birthday," *Manang* Perla thought. "After all," she had told the sacristans the other day, "it's not everyday that a bishop travels seventy kilometers to visit Tumahubong."

When she saw Father Edgar, she said, "The bishop will surely love the *lechon*."

Father Edgar himself was restless. He had been up very early and was making a last-minute mental run-through of the day's schedule. "The pins, the medals, the ribbons, the diplomas," he thought aloud, checking if there was anything he missed.

"Oh yes, the surprise number," he remembered with a start. "*Manang*, did the teachers come already?"

Father Edgar sat on a chair in the middle of the sala. He rehearsed in his mind the presentation he and the teachers had readied for the graduation.

FATHER EDGAR was ordained on May 6, 2000—only three days after Father Rhoel's death in the clearing. Tumahubong was his first mission. When he heard that he would be sent to Basilan, he felt afraid. He could have refused—he had the right to refuse—but he told others later that Father Rhoel had inspired him.

When he arrived, he saw villagers still deeply traumatized by the abduction of the children and the death of their parish priest. A year after the events, the villagers continued to remember, although families who fled last year had started to come back.

During his first few months in the village, people assured Father Edgar that they would not leave Tumahubong despite threats to their lives. "Our patron saint is here," they said. "We will not leave."

"As a priest, I could not afford to be afraid, especially with their kind of faith," Father Edgar would later say. "It is my obligation to stay. People who have no seminary formation, who have no vows to the church, are here. How can a priest whose commitment is to the people and to his vows be afraid and leave?"

The young priest was moved especially when people told him they were more afraid for him than for themselves. "Fear is always there. Even the people are also afraid. But if all those who are afraid will leave Tumahubong, nobody would be left," Father Edgar said.

Already, he had received threats to his life, even from Muslim students of Claret School. Once he received a letter warning him to be careful because there were people out to kill him. Another student told him that priests die too and have only one life. Another said that if the Claretians don't close Claret School, Father Edgar better use a helicopter to travel to the city because "they" were planning something for him.

The bandits are just around the village. Everybody sees them, even the former hostages. The bandits have even told villagers that they are angry with the missionaries because Claret School remains open. They have said they are angry because they did not get anything when they kidnapped Father Rhoel, the teachers, and the children the previous year. The victims and the survivors got money because many agencies helped them, they said, but the Abu Sayyaf did not get anything.

"Everything is up to God. It is the only thing that they hold on to here in Tumahubong," Father Edgar said. "That is faith."

ANGIE AND ANALYN were as anxious as Father Edgar that morning.

"At last, we can finally celebrate the graduation," Angie said.

Analyn nodded, barely listening to her friend. She was busy rehearsing in her mind the opening song she would sing.

She remembered the day a year ago when her Muslim students helped her escape from the Abu Sayyaf. The boys covered her with their bodies. One male student entertained the bandits as he watched the door, while the female students murmured Muslim prayers by her side.

The students later took some rags and put them on Analyn's head to camouflage her. "Ma'am, are you ready to run?" one had asked then. He also asked if she was wearing short pants, so she could take off her uniform.

Later, a male student took off his own shirt and put it on Analyn before she went out of the school. Seeing the area was clear, the students told her to run.

After her escape, Analyn realized how prejudiced she had been against Muslims. She had not trusted any of them, until the day they saved her life.

"For all that I went through and with what had happened, I thank God for saving me through the help of my Muslim students," she later said.

AT THE SCHOOL GROUNDS, the outdoor stage Father Rhoel built for the graduation rites last year was bedecked with flowers. Bright yellow draperies, a glittering backdrop, and handmade colorful paper petals adorned the platform.

Joy was standing by the rusty steel gates at the school entrance when Angie and Analyn arrived. "Good morning, Miss Beautiful," the two teachers greeted Joy.

"You're late," Joy answered. "Father Edgar is waiting for you."

The graduating students began to arrive. Joy pinned colorful orchid corsages on the students' white togas while proud parents, teachers, and guests were each handed flower bouquets.

The excited seniors—all 61 of them—came with their families; some even brought the whole clan along. Muslims are known to be clannish and on this day they were proudly marching toward the school to witness a family member's graduation. Only 18 members of the graduating class were Christians; the rest were Muslim.

The young Muslim girls were a sight to see in their colorful *turong*, which their mothers and older sisters must have prepared for the special day. In their best clothes, the families of the students came carrying gifts, flowers, and baskets of goods.

Muslim Yakan elders came in their traditional attire, which were used only during special occasions like weddings and anniversaries. The women were wearing their dainty *arbita*, a velvet, V-neck blouse decked with gold coins and buttons. They were also wearing huge gold rings, bracelets, and earrings. The men covered their heads with their traditional turbans, the ones worn only during festivities.

By 8 a.m., a crowd of eager students and parents had gathered at the school grounds. The two-storey building on the side was also filled with onlookers.

Some 70 heavily armed soldiers from the Philippine Army's 32nd Infantry Battalion surrounded the campus. Muslim and Christian militias were also deployed, with their Garand rifles, home-made firearms, and large bolos tied to their waists.

Only Basilan Bishop Romulo De La Cruz had yet to arrive.

THE BISHOP WAS READY to leave Isabela as early as four in the morning. It was still dark when he left his rented house at Barangay Sunrise. He was in his usual high spirits when he boarded the Army's Chemite armored fighting vehicle.

"Good morning," the bishop said. "Going to war?"

"Good morning, bishop," the 30 soldiers from the Army's 103rd Brigade answered in chorus. On board three Chemite tanks, the composite team of artillery, infantry, and Special Forces units would serve as the bishop's escort to Tumahubong.

Bishop Romy seated himself behind the machine gunner of the second tank. The steel doors closed, and momentarily he felt claustrophobic. The machines roared and rumbled forward. "Finally, I will be going back to Tumahubong," he told a companion.

The bishop took out his rosary and started praying. From time to time, he would peep out a hole on the side of the vehicle into the dark forest. "This is an ambush area," he said.

After Abu Sabaya aired his threat over the radio to kill the bishop and cut off his head, military officials insisted that Bishop Romy allow himself an armed escort. They also advised the bishop not to travel to remote areas, especially Tumahubong, unless it was for something really important.

Bishop Romy received his first communion "by mistake" before he was six years old at the parish church of Balasan, Iloilo, an incident his father interpreted as a sign of "something big." He was ordained priest on December 8, 1972 in Kidapawan, Cotabato. Sixteen years later, on March 16, 1988, he was consecrated coadjutor bishop of the Prelature of Isabela in Basilan. In 1989, he took over as bishop.

On the day Bishop Romy first went to Tumahubong, aboard a World War II-vintage jeep driven by Father Eduardo Monge, one reputed by the Muslims to have "powers" because the jeep never encountered difficulties on the road, he walked right into heavy fighting between two Yakan families. It was, almost literally, his baptism of fire.

Another brush with death came on July 7, 1988, on the eve of the fiesta of Isabela. An amateur singing contest was being held on the steps of the cathedral. People crowded the plaza. Bishop Romy was watching from one of the convent's windows when an explosion ripped the air, instantly killing one spectator and wounding a number of people.

"I think I grew up in Basilan," Bishop Romy would later say.

He got the nomination to become a coadjutor bishop of the prelature in 1987, through a call from the Papal Nuncio. "You have been nominated by the Holy Father as coadjutor bishop of Basilan," the Vatican's representative said.

Bishop Romy did not answer.

"Monsignor? Monsignor? Are you there?"

"Why Basilan?" the bishop-to-be asked.

"I don't know, the Holy Father has just put you there."

When Bishop Romy's superior learned of the news, he said: "Be ready, Romy. You are going to a godforsaken place. You've been dreaming of going to a mission. Now you are going to a mission in a godforsaken place."

When he first saw the island from the boat, however, the young bishop saw a beautiful green mass of land. "I wonder why they call this paradise a godforsaken place," he thought.

ABOUT TEN KILOMETERS from Tumahubong, the bishop's convoy suddenly stopped. The rugged road was too much for one of the armored vehicles. It blew a tire, causing a few minutes of delay.

At Claret School, Father Edgar was getting anxious. "I hope they're safe," he prayed. "What's taking them so long?"

The sun was already out when Bishop Romy finally arrived at the village. Children ran around, waving and smiling at the military vehicles. "The bishop's here," the children shouted.

The Mass immediately started. Both Muslims and Christians stood up and joined in the celebration. During the singing of the Our Father, some Muslims held hands with the Christians.

In his homily, the bishop urged the Christians not to lose faith in God despite the threats of violence. Speaking in Chavacano and English, he reminded the faithful to recall Jesus' sacrifices on Calvary.

"Let us be followers of Jesus and not be ashamed of that because Jesus will be ashamed if we do not believe in him," he said. He called on the crowd to "pray and hope that others will respect that we are followers of Jesus."

To the graduates, he said: "I would like you to instill in your hearts and in your minds that education is not given to you only to have money and high-paying jobs. Education is supposed to make you better men and women who think not only of themselves but also of the good of others."

"This is my wish and prayer, that you, graduates, will be able to say to us one day that you have succeeded in becoming the person that your school can be proud of. If one day you can come back and you can tell us that you have succeeded in contributing to peace and reconciliation, to peace and development, then we will be very proud of you, dear graduates."

In his seat, Father Edgar looked closer at the graduates. They were his first graduating class. Seeing the smiles on their faces, he felt happy that he had accepted the assignment in Tumahubong.

Bishop Romy went on with his sermon. Even the Muslims were listening to his every word. "Look around you, dear graduates. Look at your parents and see if they can be models for you, models in a life that you can truly be proud of, models in good Christian living for Christians or good Muslim life for Muslims."

"Our dream here on earth is that we might achieve peace and reconciliation. Peace is a gift of God for Muslims and Christians. Peace is your dream, my dream. It is also the dream and the wish of God that you and I will live in peace. And so, we are journeying, hopefully toward that peace and reconciliation. It is difficult to attain but it is not impossible."

"My journey in Basilan is about to end, but the journey will go on," the bishop said as he announced his impending departure from the island. Rome was transferring him to another diocese, leaving Basilan without a bishop.

He said he knew that the grief of the loved ones of those beheaded and killed was not over yet, the wounds of those who survived not totally healed, and their nightmares not fully disappeared.

"Father, do not withhold your Spirit from us but help us find a life of peace after these days of trouble," Bishop Romy quoted the Psalms as he called on all Christians to continue the dialogue of life with the Muslims and work together to remove biases and prejudices.

"Take extra care to be sensitive about their religious or cultural practices and study how you can best reach out to them without denying our own practices and beliefs as disciples of Jesus," he urged the Christians.

Then he said: "Like all of you, my dear graduates, I would like to go to heaven one day. That is my dream, my desire. In the meantime, I am journeying. For this particular phase of my journey, I can only thank God for having helped me to become an instrument of his goodness, of his love for you, his people. And I thank God for having given me the privilege to serve in Basilan, to be with you here in Tumahubong."

AT THAT POINT IN THE MASS when the sign of peace is exchanged, Christian and Muslim students and parents shook each other's hands. Some embraced.

Looking at the scene, Bishop Romy felt a lump in his throat.

Angie, who was sitting near the podium on one side of the stage, started to cry. "*Hay Hesus!* If only every day were like today, then everybody would be happy," she said.

AN INTERMISSION followed right after the Mass. It was time for Angie, Analyn, and Father Edgar to spring their "surprise number."

"I just hope the students and the bishop will enjoy this," Angie whispered to Father Edgar.

"I'm sure they will be very surprised," the priest said, smiling.

Then the music played. The priest and the teachers appeared on stage, dancing to the beat of techno music. The crowd roared.

Angie felt relieved that the people seemed to have already forgotten her infamous "nude run" last year when the bandits attacked. "If only *Nanay* were here, she would have had a good laugh, too," she thought to herself.

BISHOP ROMY ate a hearty lunch at the convent; he was ready to leave at around one in the afternoon. From inside the military vehicle, he waved goodbye to the crowd gathered outside the church.

"Bishop! I love you, Bishop! Bye," *Manang* Perla shouted in her high-pitched voice. The crowd waved, the children milling around the vehicles. "Bye, bishop," they shouted. Then the engines of the military vehicles started.

The soldiers took their guns and released the safety pins, ready for the long drive back to the capital.

The bishop again waved goodbye. "I love you," he mouthed the words.

As the convoy left the village, it started to rain. The sky turned dark, the muddy road became slippery, and the forest looked ominous. Inside the vehicle, the bishop was already wet. Water seeped through the dilapidated tank. He remembered the day he arrived on the island. The people had welcomed him with a ride on a horse-drawn cart, a *calesa*. Now he was leaving on a military tank.

"It will be difficult to leave this place," the Bishop told his companion.

By the time the convoy got back to Isabela, it was already dark. The heavy rains continued. Bishop Romy was tired. But he had to start packing his things. It was time to leave the island.

In 1999, when the Papal Nuncio visited him, he pleaded not to be taken out of Basilan. But the Pope's representative did not budge. Inside the car, he asked Bishop Romy. "Do you want to die in Basilan?"

"Yes," the bishop answered.

"If you want to die here, then stay!" the nuncio replied.

That was two years ago. Now he was finally leaving. The Vatican wanted him out of the island after Muslim extremists and bandits aired their threats against him.

As a "good soldier of God," he followed the wishes of his superiors. "But there's always a first love," he would say later. "And first loves never die."

IN A CORNER OF THE CATHEDRAL IN ISABELA, Manang Dolor listened intently as the bishop said goodbye. She wanted to cry. It was the same feeling she had when her friend Bishop Querexeta left several years before. It was the same feeling she had when she saw the hand of Mr. Rubio's wife sometime in the last week of April 2000, a few days before her friend Father Rhoel died.

When she learned that Father Rhoel had died, she wept. "I knew it," she said then. "He will never be able to fulfill his promise to celebrate my birthday with me."

Father Rhoel had once told her, "Dolor, I hope you will not change and you will always have the same humility. I hope that you will not be like other people who demand something in return for their services. Let us be men and women for others. Will you promise me that?"

"*Hoy*, Dolor, why are you silent?" *Manang* Lourdes asked her friend as she guided her down the steps of the cathedral. "I hope the bishop will come back to visit us, *no*?"

"Don't worry, Lourdes. He will come back soon," the blind woman said.

"If you say so, it will happen," *Manang* Lourdes said. Her friend's predictions always came true. But still the words of the bishop echoed in *Manang* Lourdes' ears: "In life, journeys must end so that other journeys can begin."

The two then started walking toward their home in Sunrise Village.

Unknown to Dolor, far from her all-seeing inner eye, there hung on one side of the altar inside the cathedral a banner with these words: "Journeys Ended, Journeys Begun."

IT WAS DRIZZLING, but the obscure light of the moon still shone on the wet leaves. Frogs were croaking in a nearby creek.

It was around eleven in the evening on Friday, June 1, 2001.

Retired Army Colonel Fernando Bajet woke up with a start. He stood up and peered outside the second-floor window of his house at the back of the Dr. Jose Maria Torres Memorial Hospital in Lamitan.

"Sinabi ko na nga ba, eh. Nangyari na nga (What I feared has come true)," he told his wife, Edna.

The retired soldier took his .45-caliber pistol from the drawer and went out of the house.

At around thirty minutes past midnight, a policeman at the nearby headquarters called up Bajet's house. Edna answered the phone. Was Bajet's brother, also a police officer, still at home? The caller said they needed the key to the armory.

"Why?" Edna asked.

"The Abu Sayyaf has invaded the hospital," the caller said.

At around one, a shootout erupted between local policemen and the bandits.

At four in the morning, the retired colonel went back to his house to get a jacket and a Garand rifle.

"Where are you going?" his wife asked.

"Outside," the retired soldier said.

Before leaving the house, Bajet made the sign of the cross in *front of the altar inside the couple's room. He kissed a picture of Jesus Christ, and then bent down to kiss his grandchild who was sleeping.*

"Be careful," his wife said.

Outside, the bursts of gunfire intensified.

"When will this ever end?" Edna heard her husband murmur as he closed the door behind him. That was the last time she saw him alive.

THERE HAS ALWAYS BEEN TROUBLE *on the fringes, but Lamitan was in deep slumber until the Abu Sayyaf decided to wake it up.*

That night, Father Loi Nacorda, who became parish priest of Lamitan after his abduction in 1994, was sleeping soundly inside the convent when a phone call roused him. "Do not come out of the convent, Father. There are armed men all over the compound," the caller said.

The priest went inside his room and got dressed. He took his .45 and ran downstairs. He woke up a church worker staying on the first floor of the convent to help him alert the soldiers in their quarters at the back of the convent.

When they got outside, the soldiers were already awake. But it was too late. In that same instant, a gun was already pointed at the priest. The bandit was about six meters away from him.

"Father, they're here. Run!" the church worker shouted.

"He's the priest. Shoot!" someone shouted in the darkness.

They ran and hid behind the soldiers' quarters. They heard the bandits shoot one of the soldiers. Another shot killed the priest's driver, still sleeping in the quarters.

"The priest is dead! Allahu Akbar, Allahu Akbar, the priest is dead," the bandits shouted.

Father Loi and the church worker stayed in their hiding place for almost two hours. It was dark and the space was too small for them, but they did not move.

Outside, darkness blanketed the town after the electricity was cut off. The ban-

dits were all over the hospital and church compound. Residents were running in different directions.

At the Dominican Sisters convent, just across the hospital, a hole in the wall saved the nuns' lives. Sensing danger when they heard someone pounding on the convent door, the nuns, who were in their nightclothes, sneaked through the hole, climbed the barbed wire fence, and jumped outside the compound.

Another group of bandits, however, was able to take another priest and a seminarian, whom Father Loi had failed to wake up. The bandits brought them to the hospital where the other hostages, including the twenty kidnapped from posh Dos Palmas resort in Palawan on May 27, 2001, were being held.

When the sun rose on Saturday morning, the bandits had totally taken over the hospital and the adjacent Saint Peter's Church. They had also seized several more hostages.

"We are part of an Abu Sayyaf suicide squad," a certain Abu Sulaiman called a local radio station in Zamboanga. "We have two hundred more hostages now. If you do not stop the military action, we will execute the hostages," he warned.

Military officials claimed the town had already been cordoned off, but added that soldiers could not move forward because the "suicide group" had positioned snipers on the uppermost floors of the hospital and in the belfry of the church.

A team of Scout Rangers arrived from Zamboanga City at around seven in the morning. From the port, the soldiers proceeded to the town center. They received orders to report to military headquarters on the other side of town. They passed by Saint Peter's Church and became perfect targets for the bandits. At least three soldiers were killed instantly.

ALMOST AT THE SAME MOMENT the bandits were shooting the soldiers, a military general was meeting in a hotel room in Zamboanga City with the family of one of the Palawan hostages.

Hours after the meeting, the general arrived in Lamitan and went straight to the town's government hospital, about a kilometer from the Dr. Jose Maria Torres Hospital. He carried a black attaché case.

In the hospital's pharmacy, the general met with a colonel. He opened the briefcase, which contained bundles of P1,000 bills, and showed it to the colonel, not mindful of the nurses looking at the two military officers.

"When will the fighting end?" a nurse asked the general, referring to the siege at the nearby church and hospital.

"It will end soon," the general smiled. "This afternoon," he added, as he handed the nurses P1,000 bills.

A FULL-DAY FIREFIGHT ensued after the ambush of the Scout Rangers. An estimated 3,000 government troops surrounded the town proper while military helicopters fired rockets in the vicinity of the church and the hospital, boring holes and burning houses in the neighborhood.

All exits of the compound were covered, the military announced. But at around 5:30 p.m., the bandits, with hostages in tow, made an easy escape.

Residents said soldiers stationed at the back of the hospital were ordered to move out for a briefing at about four in the afternoon. Eight armed civilians and a policeman, however, refused to leave. They saw the bandits come out through a small gate at the back of the hospital, and engaged them in a firefight. In the commotion, at least six hostages were able to escape, and two bandits were wounded.

After the fiasco, the public mood all over the country turned ugly. Why were the soldiers pulled out from the back of the hospital? Were the bandits allowed to escape?

Armed Forces of the Philippines spokesman Brig. Gen. Edilberto Adan said the military had put a premium on the safety of the remaining hostages.

"The [bandits] slipped through the military dragnet and they did so by operating under the cover of darkness, diversionary tactics, and using the hostages as human shields," Adan said.

"Because of the military's desire to save lives, the troops around the hospital held their fire to prevent accidentally hitting the hostages," he added.

But residents accused the military of staging an "acoustic war." They said the bandits had been walking casually away from the hospital until the civilian volunteers shot it out with them. They also wondered why the soldiers kept on firing, stopping only around five on Sunday morning, when the bandits had made their escape as early as 5:30 p.m. on Saturday.

Thirty minutes before the bandits left the hospital, however, Abu Sayyaf spokesman Abu Sabaya made a mysterious phone call. "I thought you said it was all clear. Why are you still shooting?" he was heard saying.

TO FORMER ABU SAYYAF VICTIMS, however, Abu Sabaya's phone call poses no mystery. Before the May 3, 2000 "rescue" of Father Rhoel and the other Mount Punoh Mahadji hostages, the Abu Sayyaf spokesman also made a call on his cellular phone.

A year after her ordeal, Marissa remains in hiding. There are many things she has a hard time forgetting, which have led her to understand why the bandits, despite the government's all-out war against them, continue to roam the southern islands of the Philippines.

Marissa still remembers vividly when the military assault on Mount Punoh Mahadji began on April 19, 2000. She was at the "high ground," where she was being kept by Abu Sabaya.

"What time will you attack us? What time exactly will the grenades hit us?" Marissa heard Abu Sabaya asking someone on his cellular phone.

The calls did not happen only once, Marissa says now. On other occasions, she heard Abu Sabaya talking to someone on his two-way radio, asking for details as to the exact time and date of an attack. The male voice on the radio gave Abu Sabaya specific details of an impending attack.

"There was no mystery. The bandits knew exactly when to move and when the military would attack. They were always informed ahead of time," Marissa says. During the 2000 kidnapping, for instance, the bandits and their hostages left Camp Abdurazzak midnight of April 29. Bombs rained on the bandits' lair on April 30, and later that day the military overran the camp.

On the second night of the trek, Marissa recalls, they crossed Kumalarang River, the biggest river basin in Basilan, somewhere near the village of Atong-atong. They passed at least five military detachments, but those manning the posts seemed to have turned blind and deaf. Some soldiers pretended they did not see the bandits and the hostages, while others deliberately let the group pass.

One time, five militiamen guarding a military detachment even talked to Marissa's guard. "Hurry up while our commander is not looking," the militiaman told Abu Tamiya in Tausug. (Marissa could understand Tausug). The militiaman was a Muslim. He was wearing a red scarf, but what puzzled Marissa was the fact that the soldiers inside the detachment just watched them pass.

Mr. Rubio confirms Marissa's story.

The school principal, who has opted to retire from Claret School, said even Father Rhoel was frustrated with what he saw during the trek from Mount Punoh Mahadji.

On the third night of the trek, the priest told Marissa and Mr. Rubio. "Did you see that? These are military detachments and they just let us pass. It's hopeless, we can't even trust the military," the priest said.

"I wish that the helicopters would finally see us. I'd rather that they drop bombs on us than continue with this walk," Mr. Rubio said.

The former school principal also remembers the young lieutenant who led their rescue, who was so angry when he found that the machineguns they carried had no firing pins.

In July 2001, at about the same time the national police brought Hector Janjalani, Khaddafy's older brother from his detention cell in Manila, to his arraignment on kidnapping charges at a trial court in Zamboanga, it was reported that members of the Armed Forces assigned in Basilan were undergoing a loyalty check.

"It is incumbent among us in the AFP to check our people for possible connections or links with the Abu Sayyaf. But we are not doing it just now. We've been doing this since before," a military official was quoted by the press.

The military high command in Manila had earlier announced the relief of a general and a colonel. The two had been part of the effort to track down the bandit group in Mindanao. They were not dismissed from the service, however. They were given new assignments in other areas instead.

IT SEEMS ALMOST A LIFETIME AGO. In the jungles of Mount Punoh Mahadji, hardly any signs are left of the 45-day ordeal suffered by the 53 victims of the Abu Sayyaf. The outcry over their abduction died down almost immediately after their "rescue."

For the kidnap victims, however, the gruesome drama refuses to sink into oblivion. Memories of their sleepless nights in a cramped, windowless, wooden cell refuse to fade even in their sleep.

And even as the government seems to be succeeding in its all-out war against the "money-crazed gang of criminals," as President Gloria Macapagal Arroyo likes to call the Abu Sayyaf Group, the Basilan victims find in it hardly any consolation.

They still have vivid recollections of the terror they lived through.

Along with the harsh memories are the grief and pain the victims bear over the deaths of their fellow captives, especially that of their school director, Father Rhoel. On his first death anniversary, the Gallardo family offered a Mass in Castillejos, Zambales, while Rhoel's Claretian family celebrated Mass at the Himlayang Pilipino Memorial Park in Quezon City.

The children find it especially hard to forget.

Chary says she is always scared, especially when she sees some Abu Sayyaf members roaming around their village.

Kipyong vows to avenge what the group did to him and his teachers. "Before I was kidnapped, I had thought of becoming an engineer so that I could help my family, but not anymore. Now, I just want to join the military when I grow up so that I can get back at them or their children," he says.

He was only in Grade 4 when he was kidnapped, having had to stop school several times to help his father, a farmer in another town. "My father has been struggling to send me to school, only for me to be kidnapped," he says.

He has also had to deal with a new environment, after his father decided to transfer him to another town to put him under the care of church workers. His father stays in another area, with his four younger siblings.

Rosebert still suffers from his bullet wound. He refuses to talk about his ordeal and wants to forget everything. His wife Lydda lost her arm. They still live in Basilan, and continue to teach at the Sinangkapan Elementary School.

On May 6, 2000, three days after their rescue, the couple celebrated their sixth wedding anniversary inside the Southern Command's Camp Navarro Hospital.

Joy Reambonanza, one of the few teachers who hid from the abductors with the help of her Muslim students, had had her two sons and a daughter taken from her, but they were released after five days through the help of a Muslim neighbor.

The short stay of her children in the mountain, however, changed their lives completely. "I transferred them to [another area] so that they could start anew. My husband stays with them, but it has been hard for us because we have to pay for rent of the apartment where they stay. We struggle to make my salary fit," she says.

Another parent shared the sentiment.

"It's been almost a year, but it always seems like the kidnapping happened only yesterday," says a 43-year-old mother. "Sometimes, my six-year-old daughter still dreams of the Abu Sayyaf men."

It has not helped that the government scholarships offered by the Estrada administration to the kidnapped children have not materialized.

The National Anti-Poverty Commission promised all the kidnapped students they would receive scholarships for elementary, high school, and college. Up to now, however, her daughter, who is in grade school, has not received a single centavo for her school expenses.

She says that almost every week, her husband inquires at the NAPC office in Zamboanga City, but he is always asked to come back another day. She says the NAPC even promised the students an allowance of up to P1,500 a month, but it is a promise that has not been kept.

Mr. Rubio has moved to another province. He now runs a small business with the retirement pay he got from Claret School. He misses his family. They are still in Tumahubong because, he says, "that is where our heart is."

Others have had to make even more drastic adjustments.

Schoolteachers Wenifer and Marissa left Mindanao for good. The two are now teaching in other schools.

Wenifer had lost her baby during the kidnapping. In April 2001, she gave birth to another baby. She says, however, that she continues to remember the pain of losing her first child.

The nightmare of the abduction experience continues to haunt the kidnap victims. Up to now, they live in fear. Their loved ones, too, continue to share their pain.

The government's all-out war against the Abu Sayyaf continues, but as of this writing the military has not captured all of the group's notorious leaders. They who call themselves the Bearers of the Sword continue to roam the southern islands.

And in Isabela, Manang Dolor continues to heal the poor, and still sees red on the palm of their hands.

THE ABU SAYYAF CHRONOLOGY

Mid 1980s: Ustadz Wahab Akhbar, an Islamic preacher, forms a small group of Muslims in Basilan who call themselves "mujahideen" or religious fighters.

Early 1990s: Abdurajak Abubakar Janjalani forms the Al Harakatul Islamia or the Abu Sayyaf (Bearer of the Sword) Group.

March 18, 1993: Abu Sayyaf kidnaps Father Bernardo Blanco.

June 8, 1994: Father Cirilo Nacorda is taken hostage by the Abu Sayyaf.

January 12, 1995: The Abu Sayyaf is implicated in a plot to assassinate Pope John Paul II in Manila. One of the alleged foreign assassins is arrested and later extradited to the United States.

April 4, 1995: Abu Sayyaf bandits raid the mainly Christian southern town of Ipil, killing 53 people and burning the town center.

December 18, 1998: Abu Sayyaf founder Abdurajak Abubakar Janjalani is killed in Basilan. He is replaced by his younger brother, Khaddafy Janjalani as leader of the bandit group.

February 14, 1999: Six catechists from Tumahubong on their way to Isabela for an Alay Kapwa seminar are ambushed by still unidentified gunmen.

March 20, 2000: About 80 heavily-armed members of the Abu Sayyaf Group storm Claret School of Tumahubong and three other public schools in the area, taking as hostages students, teachers and Father Rhoel Gallardo, cmf, parish priest and director of Claret School. They are brought to the Abu Sayyaf's Camp Abdurazzak in the hinterlands of Sumisip, Basilan.

March 23, 2000: Bandits release pregnant teacher Wenifer Silorio.

March 24, 2000: An armed civilian group snatches eleven relatives of Abu Sayyaf leader Khaddafy Janjalani, including his wife and year-old daughter, to pressure him into releasing all the hostages. The vigilantes are headed by Abdul Mijal, a former member of the Abu Sayyaf and now a bodyguard of the governor of Basilan. Two of Mijal's daughters are among those kidnapped. The governor, however, denies any hand of his men in the retaliatory act.

March 25, 2000: The Abu Sayyaf releases 18 out of 53 hostages. Those released—10 students and 8 teachers—are all Muslims, as well as relatives of the families of the members of the Abu Sayyaf who were mistakenly taken along with the others, including Mijal's two daughters.

March 27, 2000: Abu Sayyaf leaders refuse to divulge the reason for the kidnapping. They say that they will relay their message only to either a representative of the Vatican or to Robin Padilla, a popular actor in action movies and ex-convict who was converted to Islam while in prison.

April 4, 2000: Muslim vigilantes threaten to kill the kidnapped members of the family of Khaddafy Janjalani, head commander of the Abu Sayyaf, if the hostages are not released on or before April 16.

April 5, 2000: The crisis Management Committee in Basilan agree to allow actor Robin Padilla to join the negotiating team if he will be given permission by the Philippine government. Bishop Romulo De La Cruz, then bishop of Basilan, assigns Father Nestor Banga, a Filipino Claretian missionary, as the official representative of the Catholic Church for the negotiations.

April 7, 2000: The Muslim vigilantes led by Abdul Mijal, release the wife and the year-old daughter of Abu Sayyaf leader Khaddafy Janjalani. The Abu Sayyaf agrees to swap 15 of the 33 remaining hostages for the release of Janjalani's family. The Abu Sayyaf, however, releases only two hostages.

April 8, 2000: While the government still contemplates whether to allow actor Robin Padilla to join the negotiations or not, the Abu Sayyaf insists that no hostages will be further released unless the movie star will negotiate for the freedom of the kidnapped teachers and students.

April 11, 2000: The Abu Sayyaf threatens to start beheading the male hostages if the government fails to send movie star Robin Padilla as chief negotiator within 72 hours. Among those to be beheaded are Claretian priest Rhoel Gallardo, six teachers and two students. They also demand for a representative from the Vatican to join the negotiations. The government gives the go signal for actor Robin Padilla to be a member of the negotiating team.

April 12, 2000: The government negotiating panel composed of Retired General Alexander Aguirre (National Security Adviser of the Philippines), Fr. Nestor Banga, CMF, a group of *ulamas* and movie actor Robin Padilla, trek to the meeting place set by the Abu Sayyaf in the mountains of Upper Mahayahay, a three-hour hike away from Camp

Abdurazzak where the hostages are held. Around twenty journalists and television crew join the negotiators to cover the event.

April 13, 2000: Finally the Abu Sayyaf met the previous day with movie star Robin Padilla and withdrew its threat to behead the men among the 31 hostages they still hold.

April 14, 2000: Despite the arrival of the government negotiating panel, the Abu Sayyaf leaders refuse to start the talks unless their initial demands are met: 200 sacks of rice, canned goods and noodles, 200 gallon of diesel gasoline and batteries. They promise to release two sick children once the food and the rice arrive. They also threaten to hold Vatican representative Fr. Nestor Banga and the *ulamas* if the goods are not delivered.

April 15, 2000 Passion Sunday: After receiving two truckloads of rice and other food, the bandits freed two 10-year old girls that had fever and diarrhea instead of releasing 15 hostages as they had promised. The negotiator, Fr. Nestor Banga and the emissary of the Abu Sayyaf, Ustadz Hussin Manatad, left the bandits' camp and went with the girls to Maluso.

The bandits handed over a letter for President Estrada with a list of demands:

The freeing of three international terrorists: Ramzi Youssef (responsible for the attack on the World Trade Center in New York), Abu Haider (one of the teachers of Janjalani who is now in jail in California) and the Egyptian Abdurahman Omar (who is jailed in New York).

The freeing of two members of the Abu Sayyaf detained here: Hadjirul Ampul (who set off a bomb in a police headquarters in Basilan) and Ustadz Patta (jailed in Zamboanga for kidnappings).

To stop the expansion of Christianity, "so that they don't put up any more crosses" anywhere in Basilan, Sulu or Tawi-Tawi.

Not to allow any foreign fishing vessels to operate in Basilan, Sulu or Tawi-Tawi.

A presidential order mandating the department of education "to pass a law that allows all Muslim students to practice their religious rights and obligations in all educational institutions."

April 16, 2000: Government answers the bandits' demands: "It is impossible. We cannot grant them."

A new demand: "The huge wooden cross that has stood for 70 years on Mount Basilan must be taken down."

April 18, 2000: The Abu Sayyaf requests for a doctor and a Red Cross volunteer to treat some of the children hostages suffering from sickness. The bandits threaten to kill or kidnap every American in sight unless President Clinton releases from US prisons the Arab masterminds behind the 1993 bombing of the World Trade Center in New York.

April 19: Wednesday of Holy Week: "At 3:00 P.M. we are going to execute two of the men as a birthday gift to President Estrada." The spokesman for the Abu Sayyaf announced over the radio.

A group of bishops and *ulamas* from Basilan and Zamboanga issued a joint communiqué to both Christians and Muslims calling for peace, dialogue, solidarity, humility and justice. Bishop Romulo de la Cruz said that Fr. Rhoel Gallardo was severely beaten by his kidnappers. Fr. Nestor confirmed that Fr. Gallardo was recovering from his injuries. He had swollen eyes and a bruised face.

True to their word, in the afternoon, the Abu Sayyaf behead two male teachers.

April 20: Holy Thursday: "Since our demands have not been met, we had no other choice," said the spokesman of the Abu Sayyaf. "They have drawn first blood and they have signed their death warrant," said Col. Rafael Romero, spokesman for the Armed Forces.

In Mindanao, Ustadz Mohsin Julabbi, adviser to the Moro Islamic Liberation Front, described the executions as "cowardly, barbaric and contrary to Islam." Government sees no point in pursuing negotiations noting that the rebels daily keep on adding new demands, and continue to threaten the lives of the hostages.

April 21, 2000: Good Friday: The Provincial Crisis Management Committee in Basilan decides to resort to the final option of using military force to free the hostages.

Late in the night, the Army launches the initial ground attacks against the Abu Sayyaf camp in an effort to rescue the hostages. There has been a great movement of helicopters and military personnel between Zamboanga and Basilan.

Bishop Romulo de la Cruz, a member of the Committee handling the Crisis, explained: "There is no reason to continue to negotiate with the rebels. Every day they present new demands and keep on threatening the life of the hostages. We are praying with the whole parish community for our brother Rhoel and the rest of the innocent hostages. We have begun celebrating Easter, but the sounds of war punctuate our songs of Alleluia."

April 22, 2000: Holy Saturday: Attack helicopters and bombers initiate air strikes on Camp Abdurazzak while Army troops pursue the attack against the terrorists from the ground.

April 23, 2000: Easter Sunday: The Armed Forces publicly announces the ongoing rescue operations being conducted by the military.

Abu Sabaya, spokesman of the terrorist group, confirms the military attack. He hints the women and children are in danger because of the operation. The group still holds 28 hostages, mostly women and children.

April 24, 2000: The Abu Sayyaf threaten to behead the five remaining male hostages if the military does not cease its rescue operation. The Armed Forces continues its attack and overruns several of the terrorists advance posts and mini-camps. The soldiers press on until they reach Camp Abdurazzak, the main camp where the hostages are held.

April 25, 2000: Military troops cautiously approach Camp Abdurazzak, the main Abu Sayyaf lair on Mount Punoh Mahadji in Sumisip, Basilan. The place is believed to be surrounded by land mines, and the advance party is slowed down by intermittent rains and the rugged terrain. In a separate incident, another group of Filipino Muslim

April 23, 2000: Abu Sayyaf gunmen raid the Malaysian diving resort of Sipadan, off Borneo, and flee across the sea border to their Jolo island stronghold with 10 Western tourists and 11 Asian resort workers. Several Western journalists covering the hostage crisis and Filipino preachers who go to mediate are also abducted.

April 26 , 2000: Father Rhoel Gallardo speaks over radio. Apparently being coached by an Abu Sayyaf leader on what to say, Fr. Rhoel asks the military to stop its operation and resume negotiation.

April 27, 2000: The military continue pounding rebel positions in their mountain stronghold at Mount Punoh Mahadji

April 28, 2000: Government forces launch a final assault against the Abu Sayyaf's jungle camp. Bringing along with them all 28 hostages still left in their hands, the terrorists start to retreat deeper into the mountains.

April 30, 2000: Government troops seize the entire Camp Abdurazzak but no hostages nor Abu Sayyaf members are in sight. Abu Sabaya, spokesman for the Abu Sayyaf, tells local radio station DXRX that they have escaped to the forest with all their captives.

May 1, 2000: Camp Abdurazzak is scoured and searched but no hostages or terrorists are seen.

May 3, 2000: A composite team of soldiers and a paramilitary group encounter the fleeing terrorists. Fifteen hostages are rescued, five of them injured. However, four dead bodies are recovered, including that of Father Rhoel Gallardo. Bringing along with them the other remaining hostages, some of the rebels are still able to escape.

May 6, 2000: Scout Rangers unearth two headless bodies from a shallow grave at the Abu Sayyaf's Camp Abdurazzak The decomposing bodies showed signs that the victims were hogtied. The report gave credence to an earlier claim of the Abu Sayyaf extremist rebels that they beheaded two hostages on or about April 19 as their birthday gift to President Estrada.

The military later identified the bodies to be those of Sinangkapan teachers Dante Uban and Nelson Enriquez.

May 11, 2000: Relatives of two Filipino teachers and seven children appeal to the government not to forget their loved ones who remain in the hands of the Abu Sayyaf.

August 27, 2000: Kidnappers free most of their women captives, in negoatiations brokered by the Libyan government. Huge ransoms were reportedly paid.

August 28, 2000: American Jeffrey Schilling is abducted during a visit to Janjalani's camp.

September 9, 2000: Guerrillas free most of their male Western captives.

September 16, 2000: President Joseph Estrada launches a military assault in Jolo. Two kidnapped French journalists escape during the fighting.

January 20, 2001: Estrada is toppled in a popular uprising; Vice President Gloria Macapagal-Arroyo takes over and vows to get tough against the Abu Sayyaf.

April 12, 2001: US hostage Schilling is rescued, leaving only Filipino scuba diving instructor Roland Ullah in the gunmen's hands.

May 27, 2001: Abu Sayyaf gunmen raid the Dos Palmas resort off the western Philippine island of Palawan and seize 20 hostages, including three Americans. President Arroyo rules out ransom and unleashes the military against the kidnappers.

June 1, 2001: Clashes erupt between government troops and the bandits, who are seen in Tuburan town in Basilan.

June 2, 2001: An Abu Sayyaf "suicide squad" takes over a hospital and church in Lamitan, the second largest town in Basilan, holding as many as 200 hostages. Four of the hostages from the Palawan resort escape in Lamitan.

June 3, 2001: Five more hostages are recovered alive as the Abu Sayyaf break out of a military cordon, taking four hospital staff as human shields. Lamitan officials later say they found the bodies of two of the Palawan hostages killed by the Abu Sayyaf.

June 9, 2001: A team of Federal Bureau of Investigation (FBI) agents arrives in Zamboanga City to gather information and consult with local authorities.

June 12, 2001: Abu Sabaya claims his group has beheaded US hostage Sobero and later peddles video footage of his supposed execution, but gets no takers. Government troops recover three bodies including two headless corpses near where he asked them to look for the head, but all belong to Filipinos.

June 17, 2001: A P5-million ransom was paid in exchange for the freedom of 15-year-old Kimberly Jao Uy, according to a *Philippine Daily Inquirer* report.

July 12, 2001: President Arroyo declares "state of lawlessness" in Basilan and orders arrests of suspected Abu Sayyaf members and supporters. Charges were later filed against those arrested for the killing of Fr. Gallardo and the March 20, 2000 kidnapping of teachers and students from Tumahubong.

GLOSSARY OF TERMS

Allahu Akbar – God is great!
Amir – leader
Anting-anting – amulet
Apo – grandchild
Arbita – Yakan velvet blouse worn during festivities
Ay, Hesus – Oh, Jesus!
Barangay – village
Barong – bolo
Buyag! – God forbid!
Buyo, bunga, mama – leaf, betel nut, mixture chewed by older people
Camote – sweet potato
Cobardon – coward
Dios Te Salve Maria – First words of the prayer Hail Mary
Gomeros – Rubber plantation workers
Hala! – Watch out!
Hija – Young woman, term of endearment
Imam – a Muslim religious leader
Kopya – a Muslim pilgrim's headgear
Kumander – commander
Langgal – a small village mosque
Lechon – roasted pig
Madrasah – Islamic school
Manang, Mamang, Nang – Respectful way of calling an older woman
Manong, Nong – Respectful way of calling an older man
Merienda – snacks
Nanay, Nay – mother
Palaka, syakay – games children play
Saitan – evil spirits
Sari Bangkaw Tungtungon – a Tausug song
Tinapa – smoked fish
Tuba – coconut wine
Turong – veil
Ulamas – Muslim religious leaders
Ummah – Muslim community
Ustadz – a Muslim elder, teacher
Vinta – boat

THE WAY TO THE IRON:
From the Queen of Spain to Magsaysay's Doctor-Priest

ON July 30, 1860, Queen Isabela II of Spain issued two organic decrees that were published in the *Gaceta* of Madrid on August 5. One of the royal edicts created a politico-military government for the island of Mindanao, including a small island surrounded by the Sulu Sea, Sulu, and North Borneo.

The island was called Basilan, a Yakan word meaning "the way to the iron." The Yakans were said to be the original inhabitants.

They were later joined by the Tausug warriors from nearby Sulu, who brought Islam to the natives; the Zamboangueños from mainland Mindanao, followed by the Samal-Bajau sea gypsies; then by the Cebuano-speaking Visayans, and later the Tagalogs from Luzon.

The early settlers inhabited the coastal regions. In the 14th century, however, Muslims from Sumatra and Borneo invaded the Sulu archipelago, causing the natives to leave the coast and seek refuge inland. In time, however, they were converted and have since embraced the Islamic faith.

Because of its beauty, climate, and rich natural resources, Basilan has always been coveted by foreign powers: the Spaniards, the Dutch, the French.

The island was once a stronghold of the mighty Moro warrior Sultan Kudarat, but the Spaniards drove him out in 1637. That year, Spanish Governor General Sebastian Hurtado de Corcuera made an expedition to Mindanao and captured Lamitan, a village of Basilan.

In 1747, the Dutch tried to capture Basilan, but were repulsed by the natives, with support from the Spaniards.

Foreign attacks and continuing Moro incursions forced the Spaniards to fortify Basilan. In 1844, they built a strong stone fort they called Fuerte de Isabela, named after Queen Isabela II. From their fortress, the Spaniards invaded the heart of Moroland with the sword and the cross.

THE FRENCH were a different story. This is how Datu Jamal Yahya Abbas, writing in 1999, described it:

In October 1844, French Admiral Cecille sent the ship *Sabine*, under the command of Captain Guerin, on a highly secret reconnaissance mission to Basilan. But the secret mission became highly publicized when on November 1, Ensign Meynard and a sailor were killed. Three other companions were taken captive.

According to the Macao Naval Minister, Ensign Meynard had gone ashore on a dinghy to get some potable water. Ignorance of the language and the people's predisposition led him to commit some offense, which resulted in a scuffle. One version says that a trap for the Basilan leader, Datu Usuk of Malusò, had been prepared, but the unfortunate Meynard fell into it.

The Frenchmen were incensed. They sent two letters to Datu Usuk; one threatening vengeance should harm come to the captives, and the other announcing the seizure of the island by the King of France. The Frenchmen then headed for Zamboanga to request the help of Spanish Governor Figueroa.

Figueroa obtained the release of the captives in exchange for some 1,000 piastres worth of mariners' personal cargo and 2,000 piastres in cash. But the Frenchmen were not appeased. Captain Guerin declared a blockade of Basilan and demanded compensation for the double killing. He thus notified the Sultan of Sulu and the governor of Zamboanga.

The Zamboanga governor protested the blockade and sent two small naval vessels to fire warning shots. He asked help from Manila but Governor-General Claveria could only oblige with one frigate, the *Esperanza*, which was immediately dispatched to Zamboanga.

Meanwhile, Sultan Muhammad Palau, whom the French described as "a crafty dialectician," told the French that the Basilan *datus* were rebellious and deserved to be punished. Taking the Sultan's remark as a blessing, the French attacked Basilan with two corvettes and 160 men.

The attack failed. Two Frenchmen were killed and several were wounded. Admiral Cecille himself immediately left Macao aboard the *Cleopatre* to take personal command.

Both Spain and Sulu claimed sovereignty over Basilan. The Spanish alleged that the people of Basilan had recognized Spanish sovereignty in February 1844, but the other European powers recognized Sulu's long-standing rule over Basilan. Using strong-arm diplomacy, the imperious admiral put pressure on both the Spanish governor and the Tausug Sultan to convince Datu Usuk and his men to surrender or face the might of France themselves.

The admiral's diplomatic efforts paid off. On January 13, 1845, all the Basilan *datus* went aboard the French steamer, *Archimede*, and affirmed the "absolute independence of Basilan vis-à-vis Spain." A week later, the *datus* signed an agreement ceding the island to France "within two years upon initial request," presumably upon official royal request.

The *Cleopatre* anchored off the northwestern part of Basilan. Upon seeing the port, the Admiral became enchanted with Basilan. He wrote: "This wonderful port which some compare to Brest, but which would rather remind me of Bosphorus ... I believe I would not be able to leave Basilan without having assured my country of some eventual rights to its possession."

The agreement with the Basilan *datus* was not enough for him. He wanted no less than a formal cession from the Sultan of Sulu.

The French fleet then sailed to Jolo to press for a cession. The Sulu ruler stalled, invoking "religious scruples." The British, arch enemy of the French, sent a corvette, the *Samarang*, to Jolo to boost the morale of the young Sultan. But Cecille was not to be cowed. The Admiral was going to get Basilan, his own "Bosphorus," come hell or high water. In fact, he insisted on an agreement that had no need for the French King's ratification.

On February 20, 1845, the Sultan of Sulu ceded Basilan Island to France in exchange for 100,000 piastres or 500,000 French francs. Cecille was to come back by September, presumably to have a formal annexation ceremony.

To celebrate their victory, the French, who were still crying for vengeance, sailed for Basilan on February 27 and attacked the island with ferocity. An extract from the French official report read: "...The Malays, driven back to the mountains, were able to witness in terror the chopping of their giant coconut trees—causing the ground to tremble from the trees' enormous weight—the fire engulfing the entire plain, the detachments moving around everywhere; and everywhere they brought destruction: The heaviest possible deployment covered every point... Five hundred men at the beck and call of Commandant de Chande destroyed 6,000 stocks of rice without the least protest, burned 150 houses, razed the entire banana plantation to the ground, and felled more than a thousand coconut trees...."

The French could not destroy Basilan's people, so they took their vengeance on Basilan's natural resources.

But all for nothing. On June 30, the French Cabinet decided in favor of Basilan's annexation. But on July 26, the King reversed the decision. There were many reasons given for the King's decision, including Louis-Philippe's desire to marry a Spanish princess. Admiral Cecille rejected all the official reasons; however, he could do nothing but obey his king.

Armed with its Basilan experience, France invaded Indochina thirteen years later. Spain continued to rule Basilan from Zamboanga. In 1854, the assassination of a company of Spanish soldiers by Basilan natives resulted in the separation of the island province from Zamboanga.

WHEN THE AMERICANS ARRIVED in December 1899, *Datu* Pedro Cuevas, a Christian who escaped from Luzon and had established a stronghold in the island, helped the new colonizers in the so-called pacification campaign.

Cuevas was the uncrowned king of Basilan. Born in Bacoor, Cavite in 1860, he was committed to San Ramon Prison in Zamboanga at age sixteen for slaying an officer of the local *guardia civil*. He made a daring prison break, landed in Basilan with six companions, and through sheer courage and ability in hand-to-hand combat, rose to be chief of the island.

He was described as a good Muslim among Muslims, and a pious Christian in the presence of Jesuit missionaries. When revolutionary leader Emilio Aguinaldo sent his own brother to invite Cuevas to join the revolution against Spain, the criminal-turned-bandit-turned-supreme-Moro-leader merely smiled, as if saying to himself: "Why should a Caviteño king fight under Caviteño revolutionaries?"

With Cuevas's ironfisted control over both Christians and Muslims on the island, a civil government was established in Basilan in 1901, and the island was again made part of Zamboanga. Christian Zamboangueños and Visayans later settled in the town of Isabela to work in rubber plantations.

At the turn of the century, Dr. James Walter Strong, after serving in the dental corps of the United States Navy, had settled in Basilan. He was the first to introduce rubber in the province. He called his plantation American Rubber. It later became Goodrich Rubber Company, then still later Sime-Darby.

There were many other Americans who put up rubber plantations in the area, but it was a European who put up the biggest. Brigadier General Hans Menzi of Switzerland was the first European to put up an agricultural estate in the province.

The island became a chartered city by virtue of Republic Act No. 288 in 1948. After the declaration of Martial Law, the late dictator Ferdinand Marcos passed a presidential decree on December 27, 1973, converting the city of Basilan into a province, to help pacify and develop the troubled island.

Bangsa Moro guerrillas actively operated in Basilan at the height of the struggle for an independent homeland in the 1970s. In the 1990s, Basilan became the center of operations of an extremist group called the Abu Sayyaf Group.

FROM EARLIEST TIMES, Basilan was known as a hotbed of bandits and pirates. It was not until the 20th century that American arms made it safe to travel to the island.

Its history tells the story of a people who have been struggling to become independent for centuries. It is a story marked by violence and resistance. A historian has described it as "a netherworld intermittently lit by the fires of war between families, between tribes, between natives and colonialists, and between people and government."

The land is used mainly for agricultural production. In the 1990s, agricultural land was devoted mostly to coconut, rubber, and cassava. Copra production and natural rubber were among the key commercial crops.

Before the Philippine government implemented agrarian reform in the late 1980s, giant foreign corporations controlled the island. When the huge rubber companies left, the government helped put up rubber-based cooperatives.

Rich fishing grounds make fish production one of its leading industries. Its sea waters including the Basilan Strait, the Moro Gulf, the Sulu Sea, and the nearby Celebes Sea—suitable for seaweed farming and fish-cage culture.

The province also produces woven Yakan cloth. With intricate designs inspired by their dreams, the Yakans blend cloth into vividly colored geometric patterns using backstrap-looms.

Despite its fertile land and virgin forests and the abundant sea, Basilan remains among the country's poorest provinces. Most of the island's food supply and basic services still have to be imported from nearby provinces.

The main poverty groups in Basilan remain the agricultural workers, the marginal farmers, and the fishermen. Most of them depend on wages and salaries earned from working in the plantations.

Generally, development in the province remains bleak, because of the unstable peace and order situation, the insufficiency of basic social services, environmental degradation, and the lack of employment opportunities.

The literacy rate in the province, a dismal 66 percent, remains one of the main causes of poverty. (The national average is 93.5 percent.)

While official statistics on teacher-student ratios reflect an inadequacy, they still do not reveal the actual situation. In the more remote areas, peace and order problems drive teachers away.

Decades of government neglect and social inequity have hardened the conflict in the island-province, a crucible of age-old land disputes, clan politics, and cultural biases.

While Muslims constitute 71 percent of the population, Christians own 75 percent of the land and the ethnic Chinese control 75 percent of local trade.

The root of the problem in Basilan is land. The multinationals used to control much of it, but under agrarian reform, some 17,900 hectares of agricultural estates have been titled and distributed to some 50,450 farmer-beneficiaries who have organized themselves into cooperatives.

Most agrarian reform beneficiaries, however, are Visayan settlers, brought to the island by the American firms early in the century. The law has virtually bypassed the native Muslim Yakan and other tribal populations.

Through the years, a crisis in political leadership, drawn across party and clan lines, has plagued the island.

As in many places in the country, the clan system dominates Basilan politics. But in Basilan, clan conflict is conducted above an overlay of ethnocultural interests. The most visible contests between Muslims and Christians overshadow inter-tribal animosity and family feuds (*rido*) among Muslims in the choice of leaders.

The clannish attitude of politicians and residents has tied down development efforts in the province. Progress is shackled by the petty politics of various interest groups, which are in turn rooted in the long history of family feuds, clan conflicts, and ideological rivalry.

The deeper problem of cultural differences between Muslims and Christians demands a different approach toward peace-building.

Although the government, through the military, plays an important role in efforts to restore peace and order, Basilan's church and civic leaders believe that force is not the solution. Indeed, the military must answer charges of corruption and even involvement in groups like the Abu Sayyaf.

The judiciary in Basilan has been charitably described by residents as "ineffective and inoperative." Most Basilan kidnappers have pending charges in court, but none of the judges have dared issue warrants of arrest. What works in Basilan is the law of the gun. Those who have guns control everything.

In a province with a population of 332,828, at least 400,000 loose firearms circulate. That figure excludes weapons held by around 5,000 soldiers posted in the island.

When former president Ferdinand Marcos created Basilan by decree in 1973, it was meant to help pacify and develop the troubled Muslim-dominated island. Today, Basilan remains one of the country's smallest and poorest provinces, and far from "pacified."

THE ROMAN CATHOLIC CHURCH established the Prelature of Isabela in Basilan on October 12, 1963. The prelature comprises all territories constituting the civil jurisdiction of Basilan Province, including Isabela City, its capital. It covers a land area of 1,359 square kilometers, and its Catholic population of 83,400 is 31 percent of the total population. The island's titular patron saint is the Immaculate Heart of Mary.

Bishop Jose Ma. Querexeta was the first bishop. As he established parishes and schools for Muslims and Christians alike, the bishop worked for the integration of Christians and Muslims. He set up projects that would benefit the Muslims as he built churches for the Christians.

The Mindanao war in the 1970s shattered the prelate's dream of Christians and Muslims living peacefully together. This was aggravated by the 1985 kidnapping of Spanish Claretian priest Eduardo Monge, someone who had devoted many years of his priestly life in Basilan attending to the spiritual needs of Christians and the economic needs of the Muslims.

Bishop Romulo de la Cruz succeeded Bishop Querexeta in 1989. He arrived on the scene just when Islamic fundamentalism was on the rise and the Abu Sayyaf was born.

A Franciscan brother was abducted in 1992. Claretian priest Bernardo Blanco was kidnapped a year later. Father Cirilo Nacorda was kidnapped on June 8, 1994, and was released three months later, but not before fifteen of his companions were killed.

IN 1849, six Spanish priests founded the Missionary Sons of the Immaculate Heart of Mary, later known as the Claretians, in the City of Vic in

Spain. Of the six priests, Father Anthony Claret of Catalonia Spain, the eldest, led the congregation until he died on October 24, 1870.

The Claretians arrived in the Philippines after World War II, by way of China. The years immediately following the Communist revolution in China were a difficult time..

During one communist campaign, Father Querexeta and another Claretian priest were imprisoned. "I will never forget May 7, 1950. It was when our Father Founder [Saint Anthony Mary Claret] was canonized. On that day, Father Undurraga and I were arrested by the communists and detained in their garrison from six in the morning to ten in the evening—no food, no water, and standing throughout," Querexeta later recalled.

Because of the "miserable and unbearable" life they had in China, the Claretians decided in October 1951 to leave the country and establish their mission elsewhere. "We hiked for five days to Canton under escort, took the train from there to Hong Kong and a plane to Manila, where we were temporarily accommodated by the Agustinian Recolects at San Sebastian. Rome ordered Father Mariano Gonzales and myself to see the possibilities of establishing [a mission] in Manila," Querexeta said.

The Claretians decided to come to Basilan where the Augustinians had once a mission. The Jesuits had stayed there, too, but they did not stay long.

The Basilan mission was a challenge.

There were conflicts over land and confrontations with the military, especially during the Martial Law years. The Claretians tried to implement pastoral approaches peculiar to the area, one of risk and of trust in free dialogue with an indigenous Muslim culture.

In 1971, more Claretian missionaries arrived. The new group tried to build Basic Christian Communities for the development of the people. Work, however, was not limited to serving only the Christians. In one particular endeavor, the Kapatagan Community Development Project, the missionaries worked with Muslim laborers of a logging company.

Not long after the declaration of Martial Law, government troops forced the workers to abandon their land and property. Many poor people, mostly Muslims, were harassed by the military; some were killed. In 1979, upon the request of some Muslim refugees, the Claretians initiated a "return and rehabilitation process" for the Muslim workers.

"It was not easy to start anew after a long period of abandonment and suffering. We had to start from zero, literally, from the ashes. But we had one thing in mind, to build communities of farmers, to start their lives again, without falling into the trap of paternalism and dependency. They must be self-reliant," recounted Father Angel Calvo in 1984.

The stewardship of land, however, was just the beginning. The Claretians continued with other projects, including land reform programs, community development projects, and functional literacy. Many questioned the Claretians' motive in helping the Muslims. A lot of Christians complained that more "non-believers" benefited from the projects than loyal Catholics. But the Claretians maintained that it was their commitment to Basilan. They also started establishing Claret schools on the island for the benefit of the poor.

THE PEOPLE OF BASILAN will never forget Jose Maria Torres, the "doctor-priest." He was a Claretian brother, a Spanish missionary for 47 years who spent 17 years of his life in China and 30 years in Basilan. When he died, he was buried in Basilan, in front of a hospital he built for the poor.

Torres was an unregistered doctor, nurse, and pharmacist all rolled into one. But he diagnosed, prescribed and manufactured medicine, and healed and cured thousands, for free. He did not choose his patients: unbelievers in China, and Muslims, Christians, rebels, and soldiers in Basilan.

Born on February 24, 1910 in Spain, Torres entered the Claretian seminary at the age of ten. In 1936, he and three other Claretians went to Shanghai, China to begin their missionary work, in a medical dispensary.

When they were expelled from China after the communists took over, he left for the Philippines and arrived in 1952. He joined the Claretians in Basilan. His arrival was unheralded, until hundreds of students of the Mission School came down with influenza. Muslims and Christians alike began to fill the mission school as if it were a hospital. The newly arrived missionary was then introduced as a doctor.

"My name has run through the whole island and both [Muslims] and Christians came to me seeking a remedy for their illness. The Christians protest against my accepting [Muslims], but I tell them that a good Christian ought to imitate Jesus Christ who made the sun shine on all," Torres said in a letter to his brother Lorenzo in Spain on March 28, 1953, barely three months after his arrival in Basilan.

President Ramon Magsaysay, learning of the missionary's work, ordered the health department to grant the *"doktor-pari"* of the South a medical license, so he could practice in the island.

In August 1955, Torres built Saint Peter's Clinic, a two-building infirmary of wood and galvanized iron. When the Moro rebellion broke out in the 1970s, life in Basilan became tragic. He found himself treating Muslims and Christians and innocent civilians caught in the crossfire. Conditions became more difficult, but he chose to stay in the province.

"I, like the rest of the missionaries, have made up my mind to stay here to the end, working for the good of all, for the good of the Philippines, and for the glory of God," he later wrote. In the first half of 1973, Torres estimated that he must have attended to some 17,000 patients. Of this number, only three died.

In February 1976, a grateful people adopted Torres as a son of the island.

Still, the difficulties continued. On December 18, 1977, at about midnight, rebels swooped down on Torres's clinic. Fortunately, the doctor had sent home his personnel the day before. The rebels reduced the clinic to ashes. It took more than four years to put up a new one. On January 8, 1981, the restored clinic was inaugurated.

The restoration, which served both Muslims and Christians, turned out to be his last missionary effort. He died on May 13, 1982, from complications arising from a peptic ulcer he developed in China more than thirty years before. After his death, the clinic he built was renamed after him.